Everyday Asian Cooking

Noodles and Rice Recipes

Lina Chang

All rights reserved © 2021 by Lina Chang and The Cookbook Publisher. No part of this publication or the information in it may be quoted from or reproduced in any form by means such as printing, scanning, photocopying, or otherwise without prior written permission of the copyright holder.

This book is presented solely for motivational and informational purposes. The author and the publisher do not hold any responsibility for errors, omissions, or contrary interpretation of the subject matter herein.

The recipes provided in this book are for informational purposes only and are not intended to provide dietary advice. A medical practitioner should be consulted before making any changes in diet. Additionally, recipes' cooking times may require adjustment depending on age and quality of appliances. Readers are strongly urged to take all precautions to ensure ingredients are fully cooked to avoid the dangers of foodborne illnesses. The recipes and suggestions provided in this book are solely the opinions of the author. The author and publisher do not take any responsibility for any consequences that may result due to following the instructions provided in this book.

All the nutritional information contained in this book is provided for informational purposes only. This information is based on the specific brands, ingredients, and measurements used to make the recipe, and therefore the nutritional information is an estimate, and in no way is intended to be a guarantee of the actual nutritional value of the recipe made in the reader's home. The author and the publisher will not be responsible for any damages resulting in your reliance on the nutritional information. The best method to obtain an accurate count of the nutritional value in the recipe is to calculate the information with your specific brands, ingredients, and measurements.

ISBN 9798524295774

Printed in the United States

www.TheCookbookPublisher.com

CONTENTS

INTRODUCTION	1
HOMEMADE NOODLES RECIPES	11
NOODLE RECIPES	21
CONGEE RECIPES	73
FRIED RICE RECIPES	81
SPICED RICE RECIPES	103
GLUTINOUS RICE RECIPES	109
SUSHI RECIPES	123
RECIPE INDEX	141
APPENDIX	143

INTRODUCTION

Asian cuisine is so full of surprises and diversity! It's hard to imagine how extreme the variety is. Being the hub of so many cultures and traditions, Asia is a heaven for all foodies. And among all the Asian cuisines, the East Asian cuisines stand out for their use of altogether different cooking techniques, spices and ingredients in their respective culinary traditions. Asian rice and noodle recipes get the most attention; there is no parallel to spicy Chow Mein or fried rice served with different meats and sauces.

Considering the importance of rice and noodles in Asian menus, we are bringing you a collection of nothing but Asian rice and noodle dishes in one place. This cookbook is here to present you with the best rice and noodle recipes from all parts of East Asia, including China, Thailand, Korea, Vietnam, Japan, the Philippines and Malaysia.

Highlights of the Major East Asian Cuisines

The main East Asian cuisines that we are covering in this cookbook are the following:

Chinese

Chinese cuisine is one the most popular in this region. The people from the Middle Kingdom have a culinary tradition that goes back thousands of years. The food is simple and nutritious, and there are many sub-cuisines that you can find within Chinese cuisine.

Thai

Thai food is famous for its unique flavors and aromas. Red and green Thai curries are quite popular whether served with rice or noodles. This cuisine makes good use of both vegetables and protein with a delicate layering of flavors from citrusy to spicy and sweet.

Korean

Slightly different from other Asian cuisines, Korean food has many unique dishes to offer, including:

- Hoeddeok (sweet syrupy pancakes)
- Bulgogi (marinated beef barbecue)
- Samgyeopsal (pork strips)
- Japchae (stir-fried noodles)
- Kimchi (fermented vegetables)
- Ddukbokki (spicy rice cakes)
- Sundubu-jjigae (soft tofu stew)
- Bibimbap (mixed rice)

Vietnamese

Have you ever tried Vietnamese phở? Well, it's a noodle recipe that is fairly popular in that country. There are many recipes blending noodles and rice with broths and stocks in this cuisine. Some of the most popular Vietnamese dishes include:

- Phở
- Chả cá
- Bánh xèo
- Cao lầu
- Rau muống
- Nem rán/chả giò
- Gỏi cuốn
- Bún bò huế

Japanese

Japanese culture and food need no introduction! In fact, many Asian noodle recipes originate from the Japanese culinary tradition. The Japanese have endless ways to enjoy their noodles, some of which are:

- Ramen—characterized by its slim body, extended length, and often yellow color, ramen is well-known for being an ideal anytime meal that you can prepare in so many ways.
- Shirataki noodles
- Soba noodles
- Somen noodles

- Harusame noodles
- Tokoroten noodles
- Udon noodles
- Hiyamugi noodles

Philippines

Rich and nutritious—that's how most people define Philippine cuisine. Boiled or steamed veggies and meats are used frequently, and noodles are most often cooked and served in vegetable or meat broth. One serving of Philippine meal can provide you with all of the nutrients you need. Some popular culinary delights from the Philippines include:

- Adobo
- Kare-kare
- Lechon
- Sinigang
- Crispy pata
- Sisig
- Pancit guisado
- Bulalo

Malaysian

Geography has an important influence on the culinary culture of Malaysia; people living on the Malaysian peninsula greatly enjoy seafood and a mix of veggies. A variety of rice meals are served with curries, soups and seafood. Some of the most commonly enjoyed foods in Malaysia include:

- Mee goreng mamak
- Apam balik (pancakes)
- Nasi kerabu (blue rice)
- Ayam percik (chicken with percik sauce)
- Nasi lemak
- Roti john
- Rendang (beef, chicken or lamb)
- Kuih

INGREDIENTS IN ASIAN CUISINES

Types of Noodles Popular in Asian Cuisines

Like pasta, noodles are made from a dough that is shaped and cut into long strands. The noodles used in Asian cuisines differ in thickness and color, but the real difference is the type of dough used to make them. For instance, rice noodles are made from a dough that consists mainly of rice flour. Likewise, buckwheat noodles are prepared using buckwheat flour. The wide variety of noodles used in Asian cuisines includes the following:

- Rice noodles
- Egg noodles or lo mein
- Rice vermicelli noodles
- Cellophane or glass noodles
- La mein noodles
- Naengmyeon, soba, and buckwheat noodles
- Shirataki noodles
- Ramen noodles
- Udon noodles
- Somen noodles

Varieties of Rice

Let's talk about rice and its use in Asian cuisines. Rice is rich in starch and carbohydrates, so it is served with every other curry or stir fry as a good source of energy. The East Asian region is suitable for rice cultivation, so you will find many varieties of rice there. Each variety has a different quality; for instance, Arborio rice gets soft and sticky once cooked, so it's great for making sushi.

Long-grain white rice is suitable for fried rice recipes, whereas brown rice is good for fiber-rich dishes. However, these are not the only three varieties of rice; there are many more which are cultivated in different parts of Asia. Some of the commonly used varieties of rice include:

- Jasmine rice from Thailand
- Kochukaru rice from Japan
- Broken rice (com tam) from Vietnam
- Black Rice from across Asia
- Long grain white rice
- Short grain white rice
- Brown rice
- Sticky rice
- Arborio rice
- Wild rice

Other Major Ingredients

Asian rice and noodles do not taste Asian unless there are cooked with certain seasonings and sauces. The following special ingredients make all the rice and noodles recipes shared in this cookbook "Asian":

Sauces
- Dark soy Sauce
- Light soy sauce
- Mushroom flavored dark soy sauce
- Sesame oil
- Red chili oil
- Sichuan peppercorn oil
- Rice wine
- Shaoxing wine
- Mirin
- Oyster sauce
- Fish sauce
- Rice vinegar
- Zhejiang vinegar
- Sweet bean sauce
- Hoisin sauce
- Chee hou sauce
- Bean paste

- Broad bean paste
- Sesame paste
- Thai curry paste
- Fermented black beans
- Duo jiao sauce
- Fermented red bean curd

Spices
1. White pepper powder
2. Dried chili pepper
3. Five spice powder
4. Sichuan peppercorn
5. Star anise
6. Aromatics
7. Green onion (AKA scallion or spring onion)
8. Garlic
9. Ginger

Tips to Make Delicious Asian Noodles

Making Chinese noodles is an art. There has to be a perfect balance of spices, sauces, and just the right texture to get delicious noodles. There are many ways in which noodles are enjoyed in Asian cuisine, all different recipes set of ingredients. But there are few things that you must keep in mind while cooking noodles for all types of Asian recipes:

1. Avoid Overcooking

When noodles are overcooked, they get too soft and mushy, which does not look good. So, cook the noodles just until they are al dente or keep them a little undercooked. Immediately rinse the noodles under cold water to instantly stop their cooking.

2. Drain and Shake

Keep the noodles in a colander or anything which will let the water drain out of the noodles. When you add noodles to the vegetable stir fry, they should be soggy or wet.

3. Avoid Sticking

Usually, when you rinse the noodles and leave them to drain the excess water out, the noodles tend to stick to one another over some time. TO avoid this sticking, add some cooking or sesame oil to the noodles after rinsing and mix well. The layer of oil over the noodles will prevent them from sticking.

4. Prepare Ahead

All the ingredients, including vegetables, meat, spices, or sauce, must be ready to cook before you heat your wok. If you will be preparing and cutting the veggies while cooking, then you might end up burning overcooking something.

5. Grease and Heat Well

The wok must be placed on high heat to preheat the oil. When the wok is hot, then the food will not stick to its base. Spread the oil in the wok to thoroughly cover its base and the walls.

Tips to Make Delicious Fried Rice

When you are cooking the fried rice, everything has to go perfectly! Unlike other basic rice recipes, Asian fried rice recipes have lots of other vegetables or seasonings mixed. The rice and veggies must cook well to get a good well-cooked texture. Here are some tips that will help you cook excellent fried rice:

1. Use Firm Rice

When you add hot cooked rice to the vegetable mixture, the rice turns mushy during cooking and mixing. So, **always add cold-cooked rice to the vegetable mixture because they are firm in texture**. You can keep the cooked rice in the refrigerator overnight then and add them to the fried rice recipe. Or if you have freshly cooked rice, then leave them in the air to remove their moisture, then refrigerate for 2-3 hours before cooking with the veggies.

2. Type of Rice to Use

To make the fried rice, use medium to long-grain white rice because they are firm and keep their shape even after cooking. Avoid using sushi or glutinous rice because they get sticky and mushy after cooking. Medium grain Jasmine rice is one of the most popular choices for making Asian fried rice.

3. Hot Wok

When you add sauces and vegetables to a wok that is not heated well, the chances are that everything will stick to its base. To prevent this, preheat the wok until it's blazing hot and greased with a sufficient amount of oil. This technique also gives food a smoky flavor.

4. Use Large Pan or Wok

Try to choose the biggest wok or pan to cook the fried rice. Overcrowding a pan with veggies and rice will make the rice too soft and mushy. When you are making fried rice, you will need to sauté and toss all the ingredients frequently and requires space. Overstuffing creates lumps in the rice, which is not good. Make about 1-2 servings at a time to handle it all well.

5. Avoid Too Many Sauces

Sauces like oyster or soy sauce are too salty in flavor. So, don't go overboard with their use, especially when you are already adding salt to the recipe. Moreover, adding too much sauce to the rice will turn them soft, mushy, and lumpy, which is again not good when you are making the fried rice.

Now that you know about Asian rice, noodles, spices and sauces, you are ready to check out our exclusive Asian rice and noodle recipe collection and try them yourself. Let's get started!

HOMEMADE NOODLES RECIPES

Making noodles from scratch can seem overwhelming but with the right recipes and a few ingredients, you can take any noodle dish to an all-new level. The recipes that follow are all the recipes needed to make fresh noodles at home.

Hand-Pulled Noodles

Making homemade Chinese hand-pulled noodles is easier than one could think. This recipe guides you to the pulling of the dough into long pasta. These freshly made hand-pulled noodles are packed with chewy texture noodles.

Serves 4 | Prep time 40 minutes | Cooking time 1 minute

Ingredients
3 cups bread flour plus more for dusting
½ cup nutritional yeast
1 teaspoon kosher salt
1 cup plus 3 tablespoons cold water

1 tablespoon vegetable oil

Directions
1. In a food processor, add the flour, nutritional yeast, and salt and pulse until well combined.
2. While the motor is running, add water and oil and pulse until dough forms.
3. Transfer the dough onto a smooth surface and with your hands knead until smooth.
4. Roll the dough into a long log and then knead it.
5. With your hands, stretch the dough to arm's length and then bring ends together.
6. Place the dough onto the surface and roll into a twisted log.
7. Repeat stretching and rolling until dough pulls full arm's length without tearing.
8. Finally, roll dough into an even log.
9. Place the dough log onto a generously floured surface and roll to coat with flour.
10. Divide the dough log into 3 equal-sized pieces.
11. With your hands, shape a dough piece into a 15-inch log.
12. With your hands, stretch the log into about 30-inch in length.
13. Place the stretched dough onto a floured surface.
14. Carefully bring the right end of the dough to the left hand and gently stick dough ends together, forming another loop of 4 strands.
15. With the right hand, gently pull the dough from the midpoint about 30-inch.
16. Repeat this process 2-3 more times or until noodles are about 1/8-inch in diameter.
17. Place the dough onto a floured surface.
18. With a knife, cut the noodles and separate them.
19. Immediately cook the noodles in a pot of lightly salted boiling water for about 30-45 seconds, stirring with tongs continuously.
20. Drain noodles completely and serve.
21. Repeat with the remaining dough pieces.

Nutrition (per serving)
Calories 369, fat 5 g, carbs 71 g, sugar 0 g,
Protein 10 g, sodium 595 mg

Rice Noodles

Rice noodles are one of the most popular noodles in Asian cooking. Best of all, they are easy to make from scratch at home. You will need a steamer or wok that is large enough to fit a 7x10 baking sheet.

Serves 6-8 | Prep time 40 minutes | Cooking time 45 minutes

Ingredients
Dry ingredients
1 ½ cups white rice flour
½ cup cornstarch
½ cup tapioca starch
½ teaspoon sea salt
1 ½ teaspoons white sugar

Wet ingredients
4 cups warm water
Vegetable oil as needed

Directions
1. To make the rice noodle batter, mix all the dry ingredients in a large bowl.
2. Add the warm water and stir until well dissolved.

3. Add 1 teaspoon of vegetable oil. Stir to combine completely.
4. Coat a 7x10-inch rimmed baking sheet with vegetable oil.
5. Add water to a wok and bring to a boil. Reduce heat to medium-low and let the water simmer. Alternatively, you can use a hot steamer.
6. Stir the rice batter and pour ½ cup of the batter onto the greased baking sheet. Place the baking sheet on the wok and let steam until the rice noodle sheet is cooked and transparent and shiny, about 3 to 4 minutes. Remove the baking sheet from the wok and let cool for a few minutes. Brush the noodle sheet with some vegetable oil.
7. Brush a cutting board with some vegetable oil before carefully transferring the rice noodle sheet to a cutting board.
8. Start the whole process again for a second sheet. Working with more than one baking sheet will be useful and quicker. Repeat until all the batter is used. Brush the top of the noodle sheets with oil before laying the second sheet on the first one on the cutting board. Repeat
9. Cut into thin strips as desired, ½-inch to 1-inch thick. Keep the stacked noodles strip separated from one another to prevent sticking.
10. To cook, bring water to a boil in a large pot of water and add noodles. As soon as the noodles float, they are ready, about 1-2 minutes. Drain and use as directed.
11. To store, add the noodles to an airtight container in the refrigerator for up to 3 days.

Nutrition (per serving)
Calories 270, fat 0.5 g, carbs 61 g, sugar 0 g,
Protein 5 g, sodium 0 mg

Egg Noodles

An easy recipe for old-fashioned egg noodles. These simple noodles are made with a few ingredients of flour, salt, milk, eggs, and butter.

*Serves 6 | Prep time 20 minutes | Resting time 15-20 minutes
Cooking time 2-3 minutes*

Ingredients
2½ cups all-purpose flour plus more for dusting
Pinch of salt
½ cup milk
2 eggs, beaten
1 tablespoon butter, softened

Directions
1. In a large bowl, add the flour and salt and with a fork, mix well.
2. Add the milk, egg, and butter and mix until well combined.
3. With your hands, knead the dough until smooth.
4. Cover the bowl with plastic wrap and set it aside for about 10 minutes.
5. Place the dough onto a floured surface and roll into ¼-inch thickness.

6. With a knife, cut the dough into desired-sized noodles. Place on a large baking sheet lined with parchment paper. Let dry for about 15-20 minutes.
7. In a large pot of lightly salted boiling water, cook the noodles for about 2-3 minutes, stirring with tongs continuously.
8. Drain noodles completely and serve.

Nutrition (per serving)
Calories 204, fat 4 g, carbs 35 g, sugar 1 g,
Protein 7 g, sodium 62 mg

Ramen Noodles

A perfect recipe for making good ramen noodles at home... This simple recipe only needs a few key ingredients to make the best ramen noodles.

Serves 12 | Prep time 20 minutes | Cooking time 2 minutes

Ingredients
3 cups all-purpose flour
1 teaspoon baking soda
1 teaspoon fine sea salt
2 large eggs, beaten
½ cup warm water

Directions
1. In the bowl of a stand mixer, attached with a dough hook, add the flour, baking soda, and salt and mix well.
2. Add eggs and warm water and mix at the lowest speed until just moistened.
3. Increase the speed to medium-low and mix until a smooth dough forms.

4. Place the dough onto a floured surface and, with your hands, shape it into a rectangle.
5. Cover the dough with plastic wrap and refrigerate for at least 1 hour.
6. Remove dough from refrigerator and again place onto a floured surface.
7. Divide the into 6 equal-sized portions pieces.
8. With a plastic wrap, cover 1 dough portion loosely and with the palm of your hand, flatten into a ½-inch thick rectangle.
9. Rub both sides of the dough with flour generously.
10. Attach pasta cutting attachment manual to pasta machine and dust the blades lightly with flour.
11. Pass one end of the dough into the pasta machine, beginning at setting no 1.
12. Turn the dial to setting no 2 and run dough through again.
13. Repeat this process at the next two settings 3 and 4, respectively.
14. Coat the noodles with flour and carefully separate them.
15. Arrange the noodles onto a floured rimmed baking sheet.
16. Repeat with the remaining dough pieces.
17. In a pan of lightly salted boiling water for about 1-2 minutes, stirring with tongs continuously.
18. Drain noodles completely and serve.

Nutrition (per serving)
Calories 126, fat 1 g, carbs 24 g, sugar 1 g,
Protein 4 g, sodium 310 mg

Udon Noodles

Perfectly chewy and soft homemade noodles with a smooth texture… These homemade noodles are the best choice for any type of soups or stir-fries.

*Serves 6 | Prep time 20 minutes | Resting time 2-5 hours
Cooking time 12 minutes*

Ingredients
5 cups all-purpose flour plus more for dusting
1 tablespoon plus 1 teaspoon kosher salt
1¼-1½ cups water

Directions
1. In a large bowl, sift together the flour and salt.
2. Add 1¼ cups of water and with your hands, mix until the dough begins to come together.
3. Now knead the dough firmly, adding 1 tablespoon of water at a time if needed.
4. Place the dough onto a lightly floured surface and with your hands knead for about 5 minutes.

5. With your hands, shape the dough into a ball.
6. Cover the dough with plastic wrap and set it aside at room temperature for about 2-5 hours.
7. Unwrap the dough and place it onto a lightly floured surface.
8. With your hands, knead the dough for about 2-3 minutes.
9. Divide the dough into 4 equal-sized balls.
10. Dust each dough ball with flour evenly and cover with plastic wrap until ready to use.
11. Unwrap 1 dough piece and with a rolling pin, roll into ¼-inch thickness.
12. Cover the dough with plastic wrap for about 10 minutes.
13. Fold the dough sheet into thirds and then cut into about 1/8-inch thick noodles widthwise.
14. Carefully separate the noodles and toss them with a little flour.
15. Repeat with remaining dough pieces.
16. In a pan of lightly salted boiling water for about 7-12 minutes, stirring frequently and adding ¼ cup of cold water.
17. Drain the noodles and immediately transfer them into a bowl of ice water.
18. With your hands, gently rub the noodles to remove some of the starch.
19. Drain well and serve.

Nutrition (per serving)
Calories 379, fat 1 g, carbs 79 g, sugar 0 g,
Protein 11 g, sodium 1065 mg

NOODLE RECIPES

Chicken Lo Mein

This recipe makes a wonderful noodle meal with a real punch of flavors. Chicken and sauce are the main ingredients of deliciousness in this recipe.

Serves 4 | Prep. time 15 minutes | Cooking time 15 minutes

Ingredients
Marinade and chicken
½ pound boneless, skinless chicken breast, cut into long thin strips
2 teaspoons light soy sauce
1 teaspoon rice wine
¼ teaspoon sesame oil
1 teaspoon cornstarch

Sauce
¾ cup chicken broth
2 tablespoons + 1 teaspoon oyster sauce
¾ teaspoon sugar

Cooking
½ pound Chinese noodles

3 tablespoons vegetable oil
1 teaspoon garlic, chopped
1 (8-ounce) can straw mushrooms
1 cup carrot, peeled and shredded
¼ teaspoon salt
Pepper as required

Directions
1. To make marinade, in a bowl, mix together all of the marinade ingredients.
2. Refrigerate to marinate for about 20 minutes.
3. To make the sauce, in a bowl, mix together all of the sauce ingredients. Set aside.
4. In a pan of lightly salted boiling water, cook the noodles for 4–5 minutes or until al dente.
5. Drain the noodles and rinse under cold running water. Drain again and set aside.
6. In a skillet, heat 1 tablespoon of oil over medium-high heat and sauté the garlic for 20–30 seconds.
7. Add the chicken and stir fry for 3–4 minutes.
8. Transfer the chicken to a plate.
9. In the same skillet, heat the remaining oil over medium heat and stir fry the mushrooms and carrot for about 1 minute.
10. Stir in the chicken and noodles.
11. Stir in the sauce, salt and pepper and cook for about 2 minutes.
12. Serve hot.

Nutrition (per serving)
Calories 284, fat 14 g, carbs 22 g, sugar 3 g,
Protein 18.1g, sodium 774 mg

Chicken Chow Mein

An authentic Chinese noodle recipe, this great chow mein is made with soy sauce, oyster sauce, sesame oil and sugar.

Serves 2 | Prep. time 15 minutes | Cooking time 6 minutes

Ingredients
Sauce
1½ tablespoons Chinese cooking wine
2 teaspoons cornflour
1½ tablespoons soy sauce
1½ tablespoons oyster sauce
½ teaspoon sesame oil
2 teaspoons sugar
Ground white pepper as required

Chicken and Noodles
6 ounces chicken breast, sliced thinly
6 ounces chow mein noodles
1½ tablespoons peanut oil
2 cloves garlic, chopped finely
4 cups green cabbage, shredded finely
1 carrot, peeled and julienned

3 green onions (white and green parts separated), cut into 2-inch pieces
1½ cups bean sprouts
¼ cup water

Directions
1. To make the sauce, in a bowl, beat all of the sauce ingredients until well combined.
2. In a large bowl, toss the chicken slices with 1 tablespoon of the sauce to coat well.
3. Set aside to marinate for about 10 minutes.
4. In a pan of boiling water, cook the noodles for about 1 minute.
5. Drain the noodles well and set aside.
6. In a large skillet, heat the oil over high heat and sauté the garlic for about 10 seconds.
7. Add the chicken slices and stir fry for about 1 minute.
8. Add the cabbage, carrot and white part of the green onions and stir fry for about 1½ minutes. Add the noodles, sauce and water and stir fry for about 1 minute.
9. Add the bean sprouts and green onion greens and cook for about 30 seconds, tossing frequently.
10. Serve immediately.

Nutrition (per serving)
Calories 785, fat 40 g, carbs 75.8 g, sugar 11.1 g,
Protein 35 g, sodium 1200 mg

Shrimp Lo Mein

An easy to prepare noodle dish, this shrimp lo mein recipe features tender egg noodles, crispy vegetables and juicy shrimp.

Serves 4 | Prep. time 15 minutes | Cooking time 22 minutes

Ingredients
Sauce
1 packet chicken bouillon mix
1¾ cups hot water
¼ cup + 2 tablespoons oyster sauce
3 tablespoons low-sodium soy sauce
1 tablespoon Sriracha chili sauce
1 tablespoon sesame oil

Lo Mein

½ pound dried Chinese egg noodles
2 tablespoons vegetable oil (divided)
1 small bunch green onions, sliced (divided)
1 tablespoon garlic, minced (divided)
2 teaspoons fresh ginger, minced (divided)
1 pound small shrimp, peeled and deveined
2 celery stalks, sliced thinly
1 large carrot, peeled and shredded
1 cup white button mushrooms, sliced thinly
¼ head Napa cabbage, shredded finely
2 tablespoons cornstarch
2 tablespoons cold water

Directions

1. To make the sauce, in a bowl, dissolve the bouillon mix in hot water.
2. Stir in the remaining sauce ingredients.
3. To make the rest of the lo mein, in a large pan of salted boiling water, cook the noodles for 8–10 minutes.
4. Drain the noodles and set aside.
5. In a skillet, heat 1 tablespoon of oil over high heat and sauté half of the green onion, garlic and ginger for about 30 seconds.
6. Add the shrimp and stir fry for about 2 minutes.
7. With a slotted spoon, transfer the shrimp mixture to a bowl. Set aside.
8. In the same skillet, heat the remaining oil over high heat and sauté the remaining green onion, garlic and ginger for about 30 seconds.
9. Add the celery, carrots, mushrooms and cabbage and sauté for 4–5 minutes.
10. Meanwhile, dissolve the cornstarch in cold water.
11. Stir the cornstarch mixture into the pan of veggie mixture.
12. Stir in the sauce and bring to a gentle simmer.
13. Add the cooked shrimp mixture and noodles and toss to coat well.
14. Serve hot.

Nutrition (per serving)
Calories 333, fat 13.2 g, carbs 30.9 g, sugar 7.2 g,
Protein 26.1 g, sodium 2000 mg

Shrimp Chow Mein

These fried noodles are loaded with shrimp and vegetables. It's a quick and healthy one-pot meal you can prep and cook in 20 minutes.

Serves 4 | Prep. time 15 minutes | Cooking time 20 minutes

Ingredients
Sauce
¼ cup chicken broth
2 tablespoons unsalted Shaoxing wine
2 tablespoons oyster sauce
2 teaspoons light soy sauce
2 teaspoons dark soy sauce
2 teaspoons sesame oil
¼ teaspoon ground white pepper

Chow Mein
½ pound dried Chinese egg noodles
2 tablespoons peanut oil
2 carrots, peeled and julienned
1 tablespoon fresh ginger, minced
16–20 medium shrimp, peeled and deveined
2 cups bean sprouts

2 cups fresh baby spinach
6 green onions, chopped

Directions
1. To make the sauce, in a bowl, stir together all of the sauce ingredients.
2. To make the Chow Mein, in a large pan of salted boiling water, cook the noodles for 8–10 minutes.
3. Drain the noodles and set aside.
4. In a large skillet, heat the oil over medium-high heat and sauté the carrots and ginger for 1–2 minutes.
5. Add the shrimp and cook for 2–3 minutes.
6. Stir in the sauce and cook for 1–2 minutes.
7. Gently stir in the noodles.
8. Stir in the bean sprouts, spinach and green onions and cook for 2–3 minutes.
9. Serve immediately.

Nutrition (per serving)
Calories 330, fat 12.4 g, carbs 26.5 g, sugar 2.6 g,
Protein 28.4 g, sodium 662 mg

Stir-Fried Chicken Noodles

One of the best and most delicious recipes for noodles with chicken. The marinade gives this chicken a wonderful taste.

Serves 4 | Prep. time 15 minutes | Cooking time 25 minutes

Ingredients
Marinade
2 teaspoons Chinese rice wine
2 teaspoons dark soy sauce
Pinch of cornstarch
½ teaspoon salt
Pepper as required
½ pound chicken breast, cut into 1-inch cubes

Stir Fry
½ pound Shanghai-style noodles
1½ teaspoons sesame oil
6 tablespoons vegetable oil (divided)
1 large clove garlic, minced
1 cup cabbage, shredded finely
1 teaspoon soy sauce
½ teaspoon sugar

1 tablespoon hoisin sauce
1½ tablespoons water
1 green onion, cut into 1-inch pieces

Directions
1. To make the marinade, in a large bowl, mix together all of the ingredients except for the chicken cubes.
2. Add the chicken cubes and coat generously with the marinade.
3. Set aside to marinate for about 20 minutes.
4. In a large pan of salted boiling water, cook the noodles for 8–10 minutes.
5. Drain the noodles and rinse under cold running water.
6. Drain again and transfer to a bowl.
7. Add the sesame oil and toss to coat. Set aside.
8. In a skillet, heat 2½ tablespoons of vegetable oil over medium-high heat and sauté the garlic for about 30 seconds.
9. Add the chicken cubes and stir fry for 4–5 minutes.
10. With a slotted spoon, transfer the chicken cubes to a plate.
11. In the same skillet, heat 2 tablespoons of vegetable oil over medium heat and stir fry the cabbage, soy sauce and sugar for about 2 minutes.
12. With a slotted spoon, transfer the cabbage to a plate.
13. In the same skillet, heat the remaining vegetable oil over medium heat and stir fry the noodles for about 1 minute.
14. Meanwhile, in a small bowl, mix together the hoisin sauce and water.
15. Add the hoisin sauce mixture to the skillet and toss to coat well.
16. Stir in the cooked chicken, cabbage and green onion and cook for 2–3 minutes.
17. Serve hot.

Nutrition (per serving)
Calories 362, fat 24.9 g, carbs 18.5 g, sugar 3.2 g,
Protein 15.2 g, sodium 355 mg

Fried Noodles

A noodle recipe with only 3 ingredients! Boiled noodles are fried in peanut oil for a perfect crispness.

Serves 4 | Prep. time 10 minutes | Cooking time 16 minutes

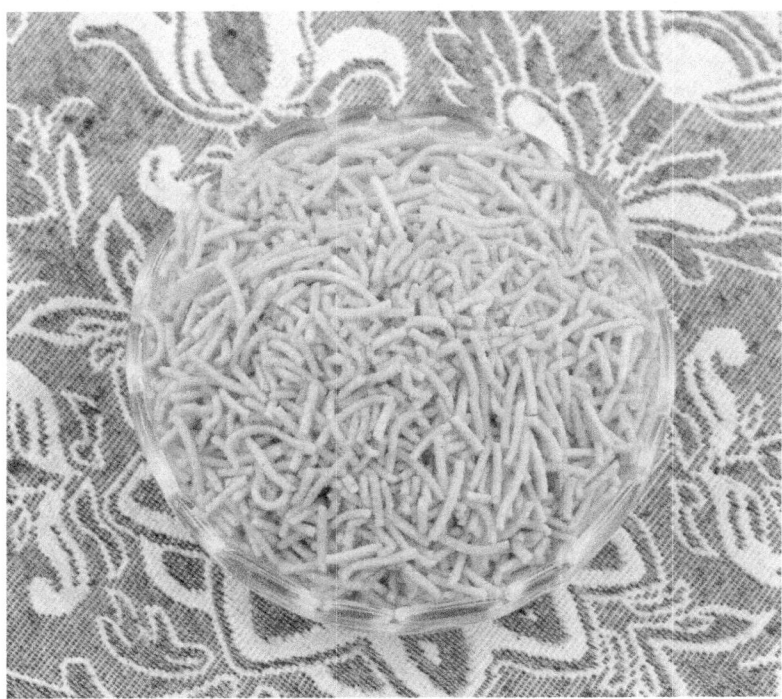

Ingredients
¾ pound fine dried egg noodles
1 tablespoon sesame oil
3 tablespoons peanut oil

Directions
1. In a large pan of boiling water, cook the noodles for 6–8 minutes.
2. Drain the noodles and rinse under cold running water.
3. Drain again and transfer to a bowl.
4. Add the sesame oil and toss to coat.
5. In a heavy-bottomed skillet, heat the peanut oil over medium-high heat.

6. Add the noodles and spread them in an even layer.
7. Cook without stirring for 5–8 minutes until browned on the bottom.
8. Flip the noodles and transfer to a plate.
9. Serve warm.

Nutrition (per serving)
Calories 237, fat 15.3 g, carbs 21.4 g, sugar 0.3 g,
Protein 3.9 g, sodium 9 mg

Singaporean Noodles

One of the most favorite noodles meals from Chinese restaurants. The flavor of this dish is quite strong because of the curry powder.

Serves 4 | Prep. time 20 minutes | Cooking time 8 minutes

Ingredients
¼ pound shrimp, peeled and deveined
2 tablespoons + 4 teaspoons canola oil (divided)
2½ teaspoons fish sauce (divided)
5½ ounces dried rice stick noodles
2 medium cloves garlic, minced
1 teaspoon Shaoxing wine
1 teaspoon soy sauce
¼ teaspoon sugar
¼ teaspoon ground white pepper
2 eggs
Salt as required
¼ pound Chinese roast pork, cut into thin strips
¼ medium onion, sliced thinly
½ medium red bell pepper, seeded and julienned
12 snow peas, stemmed and sliced thinly
½ medium carrot, peeled and julienned

1 tablespoon curry powder (divided)
2 green onions, sliced thinly
2 teaspoons toasted sesame oil

Directions
1. In a bowl, mix together the shrimp, 1 teaspoon of canola oil and ½ teaspoon of fish sauce.
2. Refrigerate for 15–20 minutes.
3. In a large bowl, cover the rice noodles with boiling water.
4. Set aside for about 5 minutes.
5. Drain the noodles through a colander and rinse under cold running water.
6. Drain again, completely.
7. With scissors, cut the bundle of noodles in half.
8. To make the sauce, in a small bowl, mix together the garlic, remaining fish sauce, wine, soy sauce, sugar and white pepper. Set aside.
9. In a small bowl, beat the eggs lightly with a pinch of salt.
10. In a nonstick skillet, heat 1 teaspoon of canola oil over high heat and cook the eggs for about 10 seconds, without stirring.
11. Cook for about 1 minute more while breaking the eggs into small pieces.
12. Transfer the cooked eggs to a large bowl and set aside.
13. Wipe out the skillet with paper towels.
14. In the same skillet, heat 2 teaspoons of oil over high heat and stir fry the shrimp for about 30 seconds.
15. Add roast pork and onion and stir fry for about 30 seconds.
16. Add the bell pepper and snow peas and stir fry for about 30 seconds.
17. Add the carrot, 1 teaspoon of curry powder and some salt and cook for 1–2 minutes.
18. Transfer the vegetable mixture into the bowl with the cooked eggs.
19. In the same skillet, heat 2 tablespoons of oil over high heat and stir fry the rice noodles for about 30 seconds.
20. Add the sauce and remaining curry powder and stir to combine.
21. Stir in the eggs, vegetable mixture, shrimp and pork and stir fry for about 30 seconds.
22. Stir in some more salt and remove from heat.
23. Add the green onions and sesame oil and stir to combine.
24. Serve immediately.

Nutrition (per serving)
Calories 294, fat 16.9 g, carbs 16.8 g, sugar 3 g,
Protein 18.7 g, sodium 490 mg

Lan Zhou Beef Noodles

A bowl of noodles with a richly delicious and spiced beef broth. The combo of warm spices is the key flavoring ingredient of this recipe.

Serves 8 | Prep. time 20 minutes | Cooking time 4¼ hours

Ingredients
Broth
2½ quarts water
1 (1½-pound) beef leg bone, cut into 5–6 pieces
1 (2-pound) beef flank steak, cut into strips
1 cup chopped green onions
5 cloves garlic
1 (1-inch) piece fresh ginger, sliced
5 dried chili peppers
2 bay leaves
1 teaspoon fennel seeds
1 teaspoon Sichuan peppercorns
5 whole cloves
1 cinnamon stick
1 whole nutmeg
1 star anise
Salt as required

Serving
1 pound cooked noodles
1 small daikon radish, peeled and sliced
1 cup chopped green onion
½ cup chopped fresh cilantro
2 tablespoons Chinese chili oil

Directions
1. To make the broth, in a large Dutch oven, bring the water, leg bones and steak strips to a boil over high heat.
2. Reduce heat to medium-low and cook for about 10 minutes, periodically skimming the foam from the surface until the broth comes clean.
3. Add the remaining ingredients and simmer, covered, for 3–4 hours.
4. Remove from heat and use a slotted spoon to transfer the beef strips to a bowl.
5. Strain the broth and discard the bones and spices.
6. Skim the extra oil from the surface.
7. Divide the noodles into serving bowls and pour in the broth.
8. Top with beef slices, radish slices, green onion and cilantro.
9. Drizzle with chili oil and serve immediately.

Nutrition (per serving)
Calories 432, fat 17 g, carbs 17 g, sugar 1 g,
Protein 51 g, sodium 180 mg

Dan Dan Noodles

One of the most favorite foods from the streets of Sichuan, these noodles are served in a hot broth with a topping of ground peppercorns and flavorful oil mixture.

Serves 6 | Prep. time 15 minutes | Cooking time 13 minutes

Ingredients
Noodles
1 pound wheat-flour noodles
1 teaspoon toasted sesame oil

Beef Mixture
2 tablespoons peanut oil
3 red Fresno chilies, stemmed, seeded and chopped finely
1 tablespoon fresh ginger root, grated
2 cloves garlic, minced
½ pound ground beef
½ cup cornichons, chopped finely
1 tablespoon Chinese sesame paste
1 tablespoon rice wine
1 tablespoon black rice vinegar
1 tablespoon light soy sauce

1 teaspoon ground Sichuan peppercorns
White pepper as required

Garnish
3 red Fresno chilies, stemmed, seeded and diced
¼ cup toasted sesame oil
¼ cup chili oil
¼ cup light soy sauce
1 tablespoon ground Sichuan peppercorns
3–4 cups low-sodium chicken broth, boiling
¼ cup chiseled chives or sliced green onions
Spinach leaves

Directions
1. To make the noodles, in a large pan of salted boiling water, cook the noodles for about 4 minutes.
2. Drain the noodles and rinse under cold running water.
3. Drain again and transfer to a bowl.
4. Add the sesame oil and toss to coat.
5. To make the beef mixture, in a skillet, heat the oil over high heat and stir fry the chilies, ginger and garlic for about 30 seconds.
6. Add the ground beef and cook for 2–3 minutes, breaking up the meat with a spatula.
7. Stir in the cornichons, sesame paste, wine, vinegar, soy sauce and peppercorns and cook for 4–5 minutes.
8. Stir in the white pepper and remove from heat.
9. To make the garnish, in a small bowl, mix together the chilies, sesame oil, chili oil, soy sauce and peppercorns.
10. Divide the noodles into serving bowls and pour in the hot broth. Add some spinach leaves.
11. Top with the beef mixture, chives or green onions and oil mixture.

Nutrition (per serving)
Calories 559, fat 28 g, carbs 49 g, sugar 1 g,
Protein 28 g, sodium 969 mg

Vegetable Chow Mein

The best-ever recipe for veggie noodles. Even meat lovers will enjoy this meal.

Serves 4 | Prep. time 15 minutes | Cooking time 10 minutes

Ingredients
½ pound dried Chinese egg noodles
1 teaspoon toasted sesame oil
1 tablespoon vegetable oil
2 cloves garlic, minced
4 cups mixed fresh mushrooms, sliced
Pinch of Chinese five-spice powder
6 ounces baby spinach
Pinch of salt
1–2 tablespoons light soy sauce
1 tablespoon toasted white sesame seeds

Directions
1. In a large pan of boiling water, cook the noodles for 3–4 minutes.
2. Drain the noodles and rinse under cold running water.
3. Drain again and transfer to a bowl.

4. Add the sesame oil and toss to coat. Set aside.
5. In a large skillet, heat the vegetable oil over high heat and sauté the garlic for 20–30 seconds.
6. Add the mushrooms and stir fry for 2–3 minutes.
7. Stir in the Chinese five-spice powder and stir fry for about 1 minute.
8. Add the spinach and stir fry for about 1 minute.
9. Divide the noodles and mushroom mixture onto serving plates and sprinkle with salt.
10. Drizzle with the soy sauce and garnish with sesame seeds.
11. Serve immediately.

Nutrition (per serving)
Calories 160, fat 7 g, carbs 20 g, sugar 2 g,
Protein 7 g, sodium 98 mg

Calamari with Noodles

A noodle dish with a seafood feast of crispy calamari combined with vermicelli noodles and dressing to create a delicious meal.

Serves 4 | Prep. time 15 minutes | Cooking time 2 minutes

Ingredients
Noodles
½ pound vermicelli noodles
2 tablespoons peanut oil

Dressing
1 tablespoon fresh ginger, grated finely
3–4 tablespoons grapefruit juice
1 tablespoon lemon juice
1–2 tablespoons sriracha
1 tablespoon honey
1 tablespoon light brown sugar
1 Serrano chili, sliced into thin rings

Calamari
1 teaspoon Chinese five-spice powder
1 teaspoon salt

1 teaspoon ground white pepper
3 large egg yolks, beaten
2 tablespoons potato starch
1 pound fresh squid tubes, cleaned and sliced into rings
1–2 cups vegetable oil

Directions
1. To make the noodles, in a large bowl, cover the noodles with boiling water.
2. Set aside for about 4 minutes.
3. Drain the noodles and rinse under cold running water.
4. Drain again and transfer to a bowl.
5. Add the oil and toss to coat well. Set aside.
6. To make the dressing, in a bowl, beat all of the dressing ingredients except for the chili until well combined.
7. Stir in the chili. Set aside.
8. To make the calamari, in a small bowl, mix together the five-spice powder, salt and white pepper. Set aside.
9. In another bowl, beat the egg yolks and potato starch until well combined.
10. Dip the calamari rings into the egg mixture and then fry them over high heat for about 2 minutes, stirring frequently.
11. With a slotted spoon, place the calamari rings on a paper-towel-lined plate to drain.
12. Sprinkle the hot calamari rings with the spice mixture.
13. Divide the noodles into 4 shallow bowls and drizzle with ⅔ of the dressing.
14. Top each bowl with calamari and then drizzle with the remaining dressing.
15. Serve hot.

Nutrition (per serving)
Calories 948, fat 67.4 g, carbs 57.6 g, sugar 9.5 g,
Protein 27.1 g, sodium 90 mg

Korean Japchae Noodles

A nutritionally balanced and tasty dish for your family dinner. The tender sweet potato noodles, beef and veggies are nicely paired with the sweet and savory sauce.

Serves 2-4 | Prep. time 15 minutes | Cooking time 20 minutes

Ingredients
Sauce
¼ cup brown sugar
¼ cup soy sauce
1 tablespoon toasted sesame oil
3 cloves garlic, grated
¼ teaspoon pepper

Other ingredients
½ pound beef flank steak, cut into ⅛-inch-thick slices against the grain
½ pound dried sweet potato noodles
3 tablespoons peanut oil (divided)
½ pound fresh mushrooms, sliced
1 cup sliced cabbage
1 carrot, peeled and julienned
½ yellow onion, sliced
4 green onions, sliced
¼ teaspoon salt

½ pound fresh spinach, cut into bite-sized pieces
1 tablespoon sesame seeds, toasted

Directions
1. To make the sauce, in a bowl, beat all of the sauce ingredients until the sugar is completely dissolved.
2. In another bowl, mix the beef slices with 1½ tablespoons of the sauce. Set aside for about 15 minutes.
3. In a pan of boiling water, cook the noodles for 4–5 minutes.
4. Drain the noodles and rinse under cold running water.
5. Drain again and transfer to a bowl.
6. In a nonstick skillet, heat 1 tablespoon of oil over medium-high heat and cook the beef slices for 1–1½ minutes per side.
7. Transfer the beef slices to a plate.
8. In the same skillet, heat 1 tablespoon of oil over medium heat and cook the mushrooms for 2–3 minutes, stirring occasionally.
9. Add the cabbage, carrot, yellow onion, green onions, ½ tablespoon of oil and salt and stir fry for 4–5 minutes or until the vegetables are completely done.
10. Transfer the mushroom mixture into a large serving bowl.
11. In the same skillet, heat the remaining oil over medium heat and cook the spinach for 2–3 minutes.
12. Transfer the spinach to the bowl with the mushroom mixture.
13. Add the cooked noodles, beef and remaining sauce and toss to coat well.
14. Serve hot garnished with sesame seeds.

Nutrition (per serving)
Calories 641, fat 26 g, carbs 74 g, sugar 15 g,
Protein 29 g, sodium 1320 mg

Stir-Fry Udon Noodles with Shrimp

One of the easiest Japanese noodle recipes, this combo of sauces highlights the taste of beef and noodles in a classic way.

Serves 3-4 | Prep. time 10 minutes | Cooking time 13 minutes

Ingredients
Sauce
2½ tablespoons dark soy sauce
2 tablespoons oyster sauce
1 tablespoon mirin
½ teaspoon rice wine vinegar
2 teaspoons brown sugar

Noodles
¾ pound udon noodles
1 teaspoon sesame oil
1 tablespoon avocado oil
½ pound ground beef
2½ cups stir fry vegetables, chopped
2 green onions, sliced

Directions
1. To make the sauce, in a bowl, mix together all of the sauce ingredients. Set aside.
2. To cook the noodles, in a pan of boiling water, cook the noodles for 1–2 minutes.
3. Drain the noodles and rinse under cold running water.
4. Drain again and transfer to a bowl.
5. Add the sesame oil and toss to coat.
6. In a skillet, heat the avocado oil over high heat and cook the ground beef for 4–5 minutes.
7. Add the vegetables and stir fry for 2–3 minutes.
8. Add the noodles and sauce and stir fry for about 3 minutes.
9. Garnish with green onion and serve immediately.

Nutrition (per serving)
Calories 614, fat 8.4 g, carbs 100 g, sugar 19 g,
Protein 27.7 g, sodium 2000 mg

Chinese Sesame Noodles

This 20-minute noodle recipe is quick and easy to assemble. A topping of toasted sesame seeds adds a wonderful touch to these noodles.

Serves 4 | Prep. time 10 minutes | Cooking time 10 minutes

Ingredients
1 pound uncooked Chinese noodles
¼ cup low-sodium soy sauce
2 tablespoons rice vinegar
1 tablespoon toasted sesame oil
½ teaspoon chili garlic sauce
1 teaspoon ground ginger
½ teaspoon garlic powder
¼ teaspoon pepper
½ cup green onions, sliced
1 teaspoon sesame seeds, toasted

Directions
1. In a large pan of salted boiling water, cook the noodles for 8–10 minutes.

2. Meanwhile, in a bowl, beat the soy sauce, vinegar, sesame oil, chili garlic sauce, ground ginger, garlic powder and pepper until well combined.
3. Drain the noodles and rinse under cold running water.
4. Drain again and transfer to a bowl.
5. Add the vinegar mixture and toss to coat well.
6. Garnish with sesame seeds and green onions.

Nutrition (per serving)
Calories 378, fat 6 g, carbs 65 g, sugar 1 g,
Protein 14 g, sodium 920 mg

Chinese Zha Jiang Mian Noodles

A favorite Chinese noodle dish. The seasoning of soy sauce, bean sauce and sugar makes a wonderful pairing with noodles, pork and vegetables.

Serves 4 | Prep. time 20 minutes | Cooking time 25 minutes

Ingredients
2 tablespoons vegetable oil
3 green onions, chopped finely
2 tablespoons shallots, chopped finely
1 chili pepper, seeded and chopped finely
10½ ounces ground pork
¾ pound extra-firm tofu, pressed, drained and chopped finely
3 tablespoons chili bean sauce
2 tablespoons sweet bean sauce
1 cup edamame beans
½ cup cold water (divided)
2 tablespoons light soy sauce
½ tablespoon dark soy sauce
2 teaspoons sugar
2 teaspoons cornflour
1 cucumber, julienned
1 pound dry noodles
1 teaspoon sesame oil

Directions
1. In a skillet, heat the oil over medium heat and sauté the green onion, shallot and chili pepper for 2–3 minutes.
2. Add the ground pork and stir fry for 5–6 minutes.
3. Add the tofu and stir fry for 3–4 minutes.
4. Add the bean sauces and stir fry for about 2 minutes.
5. Stir in the edamame beans, 2 teaspoons of water, both soy sauces, and the sugar.
6. Meanwhile, in a small bowl, dissolve the cornflour in 2 tablespoons of water.
7. In the pan of pork mixture, stir in the cornflour mixture.
8. Cook for about 2 minutes, stirring continuously.
9. In a large pan of boiling water, boil the bean sprouts and carrot for 2–3 minutes.
10. With a slotted spoon, transfer the bean sprouts and carrot to a bowl.
11. In the same pan of boiling water, cook the noodles for 4–5 minutes.
12. Drain the noodles and transfer to a bowl.
13. Add the sesame oil and remaining cold water and toss to coat well.
14. Divide the noodles and cucumbers into serving bowls and top with the pork mixture.
15. Serve hot.

Nutrition (per serving)
Calories 527, fat 22.2 g, carbs 42.2 g, sugar 4.2 g,
Protein 43.3 g, sodium 928 mg

Filipino Pancit Canton

A traditional Filipino pancit noodle recipe that comes together in an easy way. This recipe is a delicious combo of noodles, pork, vegetables, and seasoning.

Serves 4 | Prep. time 15 minutes | Cooking time 15 minutes

Ingredients
¼ cup vegetable oil
1 carrot, peeled and julienned
1 cabbage, sliced
3 spring beans, sliced
1 medium onion, sliced thinly
2 cloves garlic, minced
¾ pound pork belly, sliced
½ teaspoon fresh ginger, minced
2½ cups chicken broth
½ pound dried pancit canton noodles
2 tablespoons soy sauce
1 tablespoon fish sauce

Directions
1. In a large, deep, heavy-bottomed skillet, heat the oil over medium-high heat and add onion, garlic, and ginger. Saute for 1-2 minutes.
2. Add pork and saute for 3-4 minutes.
3. Stir fry carrot, cabbage, spring beans, and onion for about 3 minutes.
4. Add the broth and bring to a boil.
5. Gently stir in the noodles.
6. Reduce heat to medium-low and cook for about 5 minutes or until the broth is reduced.
7. Add the soy sauce and fish sauce and stir to combine.
8. Serve hot.

Nutrition (per serving)
Calories 387, fat 17.4 g, carbs 28.9 g, sugar 2.2 g,
Protein 327.9 g, sodium 1560 mg

Chicken Pad Thai

A scrumptious and tasty entree noodle recipe. This street-food-style dish is primarily made with cooked chicken, eggs, rice noodles, veggies and seasonings.

Serves 3 | Prep. time 15 minutes | Cooking time 15 minutes

Ingredients
Sauce
⅓ cup chicken broth
2 tablespoons lime juice
2 tablespoons fish sauce
1 tablespoon soy sauce
3 teaspoons brown sugar

Noodles
½ pound chicken breasts, cut into bite-sized pieces
½ pound Thai rice noodles
2 tablespoons vegetable oil
3 cloves garlic, minced
¼ cup cabbage, shredded
1 egg
2 cups fresh bean sprouts

⅓ cup peanuts, crushed
⅓ cup cilantro, roughly chopped
2 spring onions, chopped
1 lime, cut into wedges

Directions
1. To make the sauce, in a bowl, mix together all of the sauce ingredients.
2. In a bowl, mix together the chicken pieces and 2 tablespoons of the sauce. Reserve the remaining sauce.
3. In a pan of boiling water, cook the noodles for 2–3 minutes.
4. Drain the noodles well and rinse under cold running water. Set aside.
5. In a large nonstick skillet, heat the oil over medium-high heat and sauté the garlic for about 1 minute.
6. Add the chicken pieces and stir fry for about 2 minutes.
7. Add the cabbage and a little reserved stir fry sauce and stir fry for 1–2 minutes.
8. Push the chicken mixture to one side of the skillet.
9. Crack the egg in the center of skillet and cook for about 2 minutes, stirring continuously.
10. Stir the scrambled egg into the chicken mixture.
11. Add the noodles and ¼ of the reserved sauce and stir fry for about 30 seconds.
12. Add the remaining sauce and stir fry for about 1 minute.
13. Add the bean sprouts and stir fry for 2–3 minutes.
14. Serve hot topped with peanuts, green onion, cilantro, and lime wedges.

Nutrition (per serving)
Calories 487, fat 25.1g, carbs 32.6 g, sugar 4.7 g,
Protein 35.7 g, sodium 1420 mg

Beef Pad See Ew

A classic recipe for exotic noodles. The combo of soy sauce and oyster sauce gives a rich flavoring to the beef and noodles.

Serves 2 | Prep. time 15 minutes | Cooking time 15 minutes

Ingredients
8 ounces cooked flat rice noodles stick
4 stems fresh Chinese broccoli or bok choy, sliced vertically in half
3 tablespoons peanut oil
3–4 cloves garlic, crushed
2 tablespoons soy sauce
½ cup oyster sauce
8 ounces skirt steak, thinly sliced
2 eggs
1 tablespoon sugar

Sauce
2 tablespoons soy sauce
2 tablespoons brown sugar
½ cup oyster sauce

Directions
1. In a large bowl, mix together the noodles and all the sauce ingredients until evenly coated.
2. Set aside for 5–10 minutes.
3. Heat wok over medium-high heat and add oil and broccoli. Sauté for 3 minutes until it starts to wilt. Add garlic and sauté for another minute.
4. Add the beef and cook for about 2-4 minutes. Remove from skillet and set aside.
5. Add the noodles and sauce mixture to the skillet. Press to one side.
6. On the free side of the wok, crack the eggs and scramble quickly. Once scrambled, mix eggs with noodles Add the cooked broccoli and beef and toss together. Cook for 2-3 minutes.
7. Serve hot.

Nutrition (per serving)
Calories 566, fat 29.2 g, carbs 48.5 g, sugar 15.4 g,
Protein 29.7 g, sodium 1920 mg

Mongolian Chicken Noodles

One of the best udon noodle recipes for your dining table. Chicken and broccoli complement noodles in a nice way.

Serves 4 | Prep. time 15 minutes | Cooking time 8 minutes

Ingredients
4 teaspoons vegetable oil
2 boneless skinless chicken breasts, sliced thinly crosswise
1 pound udon noodles
4 cups frozen mixed Asian vegetables, thawed
⅓ cup water
1 tablespoon low-sodium soy sauce
1 tablespoon hoisin sauce
¼ teaspoon pepper
4 cloves garlic, minced
1 red finger chili pepper, sliced thinly

Directions
1. In a large nonstick skillet, heat 1 tablespoon of the oil over medium-high heat and sear the chicken slices for about 5 minutes or until golden brown.

2. Meanwhile, in a large pot of boiling water, cook the udon noodles and Asian vegetables for about -4 minutes.
3. Drain the noodles and broccoli completely and set aside.
4. In a bowl, mix together the water, soy sauce, hoisin sauce and pepper.
5. With a slotted spoon, transfer the chicken slices to a plate. Set aside.
6. In the same skillet, heat the remaining oil over medium-high heat and sauté the garlic and chili for about 30 seconds.
7. Add the chicken slices, cooked noodles and broccoli, and sauce mixture. Stir fry for about 2 minutes.
8. Serve hot.

Nutrition (per serving)
Calories 576, fat 11.3 g, carbs 74.1 g, sugar 2.9 g,
Protein 35.9 g, sodium 389mg

Malaysian KI-Hokkien Mee Noodles

A richly flavored and delish recipe for noodles. Fatty pork belly is the main ingredient flavoring this recipe.

Serves 6 | Prep. time 20 minutes | Cooking time 40 minutes

Ingredients
¾ pound skin-on fatty pork belly (divided)
½ teaspoon salt
½ cup + 2 tablespoons water (divided)
⅔ cup low-sodium chicken broth
3 tablespoons Thai black soy sauce
2 tablespoons Thai sweet soy sauce
1 tablespoon Thai thin soy sauce
2 tablespoons oyster sauce
½ teaspoon sesame oil
¼ teaspoon ground white pepper
6 teaspoons vegetable oil (divided)
½ pound shrimp, peeled and deveined
3 cloves garlic, chopped finely
2½ cups green cabbage, shredded
2 cups Napa cabbage, shredded
1 tablespoon Shaoxing wine

1 pound Hokkien noodles
2 tablespoons cornstarch

Directions
1. Cut the pork belly in half lengthwise.
2. Divide the lean part from the fattier part attached to the skin.
3. Cut the lean part of the pork belly into ⅛-inch slices.
4. Trim the fatty part of the pork belly, remove the skin, and cut the fat into small chunks.
5. In a cast-iron skillet, simmer the fatty pork belly chunks, ½ teaspoon salt and ½ cup of water over medium heat for about 10 minutes.
6. Reduce heat to low and simmer for about 15 minutes, stirring occasionally.
7. With a slotted spoon, transfer the pork pieces onto a paper-towel-lined plate.
8. Reserve the pork lard from the skillet.
9. In a bowl, mix together the broth, all sauces, sesame oil and white pepper. Set aside.
10. In a skillet, heat 2 teaspoons of oil over medium-high heat and sear the lean pork belly for 3–5 minutes or until browned.
11. With a slotted spoon, transfer the pork belly to a plate. Set aside.
12. In the same skillet, heat 2 teaspoons of oil over medium-high heat and sear the shrimp for about 1 minute.
13. With a slotted spoon, transfer the shrimp to a plate. Set aside.
14. In the same skillet, heat the remaining oil over medium heat and sauté the garlic for about 10 seconds.
15. Add both kinds of cabbage and stir fry for 30–60 seconds.
16. Stir in the wine.
17. Add the noodles and toss to combine.
18. Stir in the sauce mixture.
19. Cook for 1–2 minutes, stirring occasionally.
20. In a small bowl, dissolve the cornstarch in the remaining water.
21. Stir the cooked pork belly and the shrimp into the skillet.
22. Stir in the cornstarch mixture and cook for 1–2 minutes, stirring continuously.
23. Serve hot topped with crispy pork pieces.

Nutrition (per serving)
Calories 491, fat 22.5 g, carbs 27.1 g, sugar 2.3 g,
Protein 40.2 g, sodium 1900 mg

Taiwanese Beef Noodles Soup

A recipe for a soup that is considered to be Taiwan's national dish. This beef noodle soup is the ultimate comfort food to keep you warm during winter.

Serves 6 | Prep. time 15 minutes | Cooking time 40 minutes

Ingredients
1 teaspoon vegetable oil
1 pound beef stew meat, cubed
1 cup celery, chopped
1 cup onion, chopped
2½ cups frozen egg noodles
1 cup carrot, peeled and chopped
¼ cup beef bouillon granules
¼ teaspoon dried parsley
Pinch of pepper
5¾ cups water

Directions
1. In a large pan, heat the oil over medium-high heat and sear the stew meat, celery and onion for about 5 minutes.
2. Stir in the remaining ingredients and bring to a boil.
3. Reduce heat to low and simmer, covered, for about 30 minutes.
4. Serve hot.

Nutrition (per serving)
Calories 258, fat 6.9 g, carbs 21 g, sugar 2.3 g,
Protein 25.5 g, sodium 136 mg

Chinese Beef Noodles Soup

One of the favorite soups from Chinese cuisine, this is a great choice for chilly winter meals.

Serves 6 | Prep. time 15 minutes | Cooking time 2¼ hours

Ingredients
2 tablespoons vegetable oil
½ pound stewing beef, cubed
4 green onions, sliced
1 (1-inch) piece fresh ginger, sliced
2 cloves garlic, crushed
1 splash dry sherry or rice wine
Salt and pepper as required
1 quart beef broth
1 cinnamon stick
1 star anise
½ teaspoon Chinese five-spice powder
½ pound Chinese noodles
2 tablespoons low-sodium dark soy sauce
1 tablespoon light soy sauce
1 tablespoon oyster sauce
1 tablespoon fish sauce

6 bok choy leaves
6 Chinese cabbage leaves, shredded

Directions
1. In a large pan, heat the oil over high heat and cook the beef, green onions, ginger and garlic for 4–5 minutes or until browned completely, stirring frequently.
2. Stir in the sherry, salt and pepper and cook for about 1 minute, stirring continuously.
3. Stir in the broth, cinnamon stick, star anise and five-spice powder and bring to a boil.
4. Reduce heat to low and simmer, covered, for 1–2 hours.
5. Meanwhile, in a pan of boiling water, cook the noodles according to the package instructions.
6. Uncover the pan and discard the ginger, garlic slices and whole spices.
7. Stir in all of the sauces and bring back to a boil over medium-high heat.
8. Add the bok choy and cabbage and cook for 2–3 minutes.
9. Drain the noodles completely and divide into serving bowls.
10. Top with the soup mixture and serve hot.

Nutrition (per serving)
Calories 204, fat 8.7 g, carbs 13.1 g, sugar 2.2 g,
Protein 17.8 g, sodium 1200 mg

Thai Drunken Noodles

Saucy is spiced just rice, this noodle recipe from Thailand is so satisfying and a favorite you will be making often!

Serves 2–4 | Prep. time 5 minutes | Cooking time 8–10 minutes

Ingredients
½ pound wide rice noodles

Sauce
1 tablespoon fish sauce
1 tablespoon soy sauce

1 teaspoon oyster sauce
1 teaspoon Shaoxing wine
2 teaspoons palm sugar or brown sugar
1 ½ teaspoons cornstarch

Paste
2 Thai bird's eye chilies
6 cloves garlic
1 shallot, chopped
2 teaspoons shrimp paste
1 tablespoon vegetable oil, divided

Other ingredients
8 ounces boneless chicken breast or thigh, sliced thin
2 garlic cloves, minced
¼ teaspoon grated fresh ginger
1 shallot, sliced 3 baby corns, sliced
6 mini corns, sliced
¾ cup red and green bell pepper, sliced thin
1-2 tablespoons vegetable oil, if needed
½ cup fresh Thai basil leaves, packed
Salt and white pepper to taste

Directions
1. Cook the noodles according to package direction. Drain and set aside.
2. Whisk together the sauce ingredients until smooth and set aside.
3. Crush/pound the Thai chilies, garlic, shallots, and shrimp paste using a mortar and pestle to make a fine paste. Add ½ tablespoon of vegetable oil, and combine.
4. Heat the remaining oil over medium heat in a deep saucepan or wok.
5. Add the paste and cook for 10-20 seconds until fragrant.
6. Increase heat to medium-high. Add the chicken and stir-fry for 1–2 minutes until evenly brown.
7. Add the shallot, garlic, and ginger. Stir-fry for 30 seconds. Add baby corn and peppers. Stir-fry for 1-2 minutes. Add more vegetable oil if necessary.
8. Add reserved sauce to the wok Stir to combine for 30 seconds.
9. Mix in the noodles and season to taste with salt and pepper.
10. Add the basil and cook for 30 seconds.
11. Serve warm.

Nutrition (per serving)
Calories 441, fat 9 g, carbs 64 g, sugar 17 g,
Protein 26 g, sodium 1028 mg

Beef Pho

One of the most popular soups from Vietnam, Pho has a rich broth that is made from scratch and so deep with flavors. A wholesome and nutritious soup recipe to do over and over again.

Serves 4 | Prep. time 20 minutes | Cooking time 8 hours

Ingredients
4 pounds beef soup bones
1 large onion, unpeeled, halved
5 thumbs fresh ginger, cleaned and peeled
1 tablespoon salt
2 pods star anise

2 ½ tablespoons fish sauce
4 quarts water
1 (8-ounce) package dried rice noodles
1 ½ pounds beef sirloin, very thinly sliced
½ cup cilantro, chopped
Green onion, chopped
1 ½ cups bean sprouts
Thai basil
4 wedges fresh lime
Hoisin sauce, Sriracha, and Nước Mắm (Fish Sauce)

Directions
1. Preheat the oven to 425°F.
2. Arrange the beef bones and onion on a baking sheet and bake for 1 hour, removing the onion after about 45 minutes. It should be roasted but soft.
3. Remove the bones after about 1 hour, or when they are nicely browned.
4. Pour 4 quarts of water into a large pot. Add the bones, onion, ginger, salt, star anise, and fish sauce. Bring to a boil.
5. Reduce the heat to low and simmer for 6 to 10 hours. Strain the broth into another pot and set it aside.
6. Soak the rice noodles in lukewarm water for 1 hour.
7. Transfer the pre-soaked noodles to a pot of boiling water. Continue boiling for one minute. Drain the noodles and distribute them among the serving bowls.
8. Reheat the broth to a simmer.
9. Meanwhile, top the noodles in the bowls with the raw sirloin, cilantro, and green onion.
10. Pour the hot broth into bowls. Wait for beef to "cook" in the broth and lose its pink coloring. This will take a few minutes.
11. Serve with bean sprouts, Thai basil, and lime wedges. Offer hoisin sauce, sriracha and/or Nước Mắm (fish sauce) as condiments.

Chinese Hot Sauce Noodles

A classically delicious plate of noodles that's beautifully flavored with a combo of chili oil, seasoned soy sauce and tomato sauce.

Serves 4 | Prep. time 20 minutes | Cooking time 57 minutes

Ingredients
Chili Oil
1 bulb garlic, grated
2 tablespoons soy sauce
2 cups peanut oil
½ cup Chinese chili powder
¼ cup white sesame seeds
1 teaspoon ground cumin
1 teaspoon ground coriander
2 dried bay leaves
2 star anises
2 tablespoon ground Sichuan peppercorns

Soy Sauce
¾ cup soy sauce
¼ cup water
1 tablespoon light brown sugar
2 teaspoon whole Sichuan peppercorns
1 star anise
½ cinnamon stick
2 whole cloves
⅓ cup black vinegar

Tomato Sauce
1 tablespoon peanut oil
3 tomatoes, chopped
3 tablespoons tomato paste

Noodles
7 ounces dried noodles
2 green onions, chopped

Directions
1. To make the chili oil, in a small bowl, mix together the garlic and soy sauce. Set aside.
2. In a large skillet, cook the peanut oil, chili powder, sesame seeds, cumin, coriander, bay leaves and star anise over medium-low heat for 3–4 minutes, stirring frequently.
3. Stir in the ground peppercorns and cook for 10–20 seconds, stirring continuously.
4. Add the garlic mixture and stir gently to combine.
5. Remove from heat and transfer the chili to a heatproof bowl.
6. Set aside to cool.
7. Once cool, discard the bay leaves and star anise.
8. Set aside for about 2 hours before using.
9. To make the soy sauce, in a small saucepan, bring all of the soy sauce ingredients except for the vinegar to a gentle simmer over medium-low heat.
10. Reduce heat to low and simmer for about 15 minutes.
11. Remove from heat and strain the seasoned soy sauce into a heatproof bowl.
12. Mix in the black vinegar.
13. Set aside to cool before using.
14. To make the tomato sauce, in a medium skillet, heat the oil over medium heat and cook the tomatoes and tomato paste for 5–7 minutes, crushing the tomatoes with the back of the spoon.
15. Transfer the tomato sauce to a bowl and set aside.
16. In a large pan of boiling water, cook the noodles for 8–10 minutes.

17. Drain the noodles and rinse under cold running water.
18. Drain again and transfer to a bowl.
19. Add the chili oil, tomato sauce and seasoned soy sauce and toss to coat well.
20. Serve immediately garnished with green onion.

Nutrition (per serving)
Calories 454, fat 26 g, carbs 44.9 g, sugar 9.6 g,
Protein 20 g, sodium 2500 mg

CONGEE RECIPES

Simple Congee

An authentic Chinese breakfast bowl, this simple porridge is made by boiling rice in a great deal of water until it breaks down into a pudding-like consistency.

Serves 6 | Prep. time 10 minutes | Cooking time 1¾ hours

Ingredients
2 quarts water
¾ cup long-grain rice, rinsed, soaked for 30 minutes, and drained
1 teaspoon salt

Directions
1. In a large Dutch oven, bring the water and rice to a boil over high heat.
2. Reduce heat to medium-low and cook, covered, for 1½–1¾ hours, stirring occasionally.
3. Stir in the salt and remove from heat.

4. Serve with your favorite topping.

Nutrition (per serving)
Calories 84, fat 0.2 g, carbs 18.5 g, sugar 0 g,
Protein 1.7 g, sodium 396 mg

Chicken Congee

An incredibly nourishing and delicious breakfast porridge, this easy to make porridge gets its taste from chicken and ginger.

Serves 6 | Prep. time 15 minutes | Cooking time 1 hour 5 minutes

Ingredients
2 quarts water
1 cup long-grain white rice, rinsed and drained
6 bone-in chicken thighs
1 (1-inch) piece fresh ginger, sliced into large pieces
Salt as required

Directions
1. In a large Dutch oven, bring the water, rice, chicken thighs and ginger to a boil over high heat.
2. Reduce heat to medium-low and cook, covered, for about 1 hour, stirring occasionally.
3. With a slotted spoon, transfer the chicken thighs into a bowl.
4. With 2 forks, shred the meat. Discard the bones.
5. Stir the shredded meat and salt into the rice mixture.
6. Serve with your favorite topping.

Nutrition (per serving)
Calories 328, fat 8.6 g, carbs 247 g, sugar 0 g,
Protein 35 g, sodium 136 mg

Pork Meatballs Congee

A bowl of soothing and delicious breakfast congee for the whole family. These meatballs are simply flavored with fish sauce and soy sauce.

Serves 6 | Prep. time 20 minutes | Cooking time 40 minutes

Ingredients
½ pound ground pork
2 tablespoons fish sauce
1 tablespoon soy sauce
White pepper as required
2 quarts chicken broth
1 cup jasmine rice
1 stalk lemongrass, cut into 3-inch pieces and crushed
5 dried Thai bird's-eye chilies, stemmed
¼ cup vegetable oil
5 cloves garlic, sliced thinly
¼ cup distilled white vinegar
1 Serrano chili, seeded and minced
½ teaspoon sugar

Directions

1. In a bowl, mix the pork, fish sauce, soy sauce and a pinch of white pepper until well combined.
2. Set aside for 15–30 minutes.
3. In a cast-iron pan, bring the broth, rice and lemongrass pieces to a boil over medium-high heat.
4. Reduce heat to low and simmer, partially covered, for about 25 minutes.
5. Meanwhile, heat a small skillet over medium heat and toast the dried chilies for about 3 minutes, stirring continuously.
6. Transfer the dried chilies to a spice grinder and grind until roughly powdered.
7. Wipe out the skillet with paper towels.
8. In the same skillet, heat the oil over low heat and cook the garlic for about 10 minutes or until caramelized.
9. Transfer the garlic oil into a small bowl and set aside.
10. In another small bowl, stir together the vinegar, Serrano chili and sugar until the sugar is dissolved.
11. With a small ice cream scoop, make 1-inch meatballs from the pork mixture.
12. Remove the lemongrass from the rice mixture and drop in the meatballs.
13. Increase heat to medium-high and simmer, covered, for about 10 minutes, stirring occasionally.
14. Serve hot with your favorite topping.

Nutrition (per serving)

Calories 304, fat 12.3 g, carbs 27.2 g, sugar 1.8 g,
Protein 19.1 g, sodium 1564 mg

Fish Congee

This popular breakfast porridge is a perfect choice, particularly when you feel under the weather. This authentic Chinese congee is flavored with fish, ginger and parsley.

Serves 4 | Prep. time 15 minutes | Cooking time 50 minutes

Ingredients
3 quarts water
1½ cups medium-grain rice
5 ounces white fish, cut into small chunks
1 green onion, sliced
1 (3-inch) piece fresh ginger, thinly sliced
2 teaspoons chicken bouillon granules
½ teaspoon pepper
3 tablespoons fresh parsley, chopped
Salt as required

Directions
1. In a large pan, bring the water and rice to a boil over high heat.
2. Boil for about 5 minutes, then reduce heat to medium-low and simmer for about 30 minutes.

3. In a bowl, stir together the fish, green onion, ginger, chicken bouillon granules and pepper.
4. Refrigerate to marinate for about 15 minutes.
5. After cooking the rice for 30 minutes, add the fish mixture and continue simmering for about 20 minutes more.
6. Stir in the parsley and salt and serve hot.

Nutrition (per serving)
Calories 139, fat 1.3 g, carbs 20.6 g, sugar 0.1 g,
Protein 10.2 g, sodium 210 mg

FRIED RICE RECIPES

Fried Rice

A basic traditional fried rice recipe for your dining table. This fried rice is really easy to prepare at home.

Serves 4 | Prep. time 10 minutes | Cooking time 7 minutes

Ingredients
2 large eggs
1 teaspoon salt
Pepper as required
3 tablespoons canola oil (divided)
4 cups 1-day old leftover cooked white rice
1–2 tablespoons light soy sauce
1–2 green onions, chopped

Directions
1. In a bowl, lightly beat the eggs, salt and pepper.

2. In a skillet, heat 1 tablespoon of the oil over medium-high heat. Cook the egg mixture for 2–3 minutes, stirring continuously.
3. Transfer the scrambled eggs to a plate and set aside.
4. Wipe out the skillet with paper towels.
5. In the same skillet, heat the remaining oil over medium heat and stir-fry the cooked rice for 1–2 minutes.
6. Stir in the soy sauce.
7. Stir in the scrambled egg.
8. Stir in the green onion.
9. Serve hot.

Nutrition (per serving)
Calories 314, fat 13.4 g, carbs 40.3 g, sugar 0.4 g,
Protein 7.1 g, sodium 93 mg

Chicken Fried Rice

A great chicken fried rice recipe that is the comfort dish of Chinese cuisine. This fried rice recipe will be well-loved in any house.

Serves 4 | Prep. time 15 minutes | Cooking time 13 minutes

Ingredients
2 eggs
1–2 tablespoons oyster sauce
Salt as required
4 tablespoons vegetable oil (divided)
1 medium onion, chopped
½ cup peas
4 cups cooked rice, cooled
1–2 tablespoons soy sauce
Pepper as required
½ pound cooked chicken, chopped
1 green onion, chopped

Directions
1. In a small bowl, beat the eggs with a dash of oyster sauce and a pinch of salt. Set aside.
2. In a skillet, heat 1 tablespoon of oil over medium-high heat and cook the egg mixture for 2–3 minutes, stirring continuously.
3. Transfer the scrambled eggs onto a plate and set aside.
4. Wipe out the skillet with paper towels.
5. In the same skillet, heat 1 tablespoon of oil over high heat and sauté the onion for 2–3 minutes.
6. Transfer the onion onto a plate.
7. In the same skillet, heat 1 tablespoon of oil over high heat and sauté the green peas for 1–2 minutes.
8. Transfer the peas onto a plate.
9. In the same skillet, heat the remaining oil over medium heat and sauté the cooked rice for 1–2 minutes.
10. Stir in the oyster sauce, soy sauce, salt and pepper and stir fry for about 1 minute.
11. Stir in the chicken, eggs, onion and green peas and stir fry for 1–2 minutes.
12. Stir in the green onion.
13. Serve hot.

Nutrition (per serving)
Calories 449, fat 18 g, carbs 45.5 g, sugar 2.6 g,
Protein 24.6 g, sodium 324 mg

Vietnamese Fried Rice

A fried rice recipe that has milder flavors because of its seasonings, this is a comforting combo of Chinese sausage, barbecued pork, fish sauce and lime juice.

Serves 4 | Prep. time 15 minutes | Cooking time 10 minutes

Ingredients
2 eggs
1⅛ teaspoons fish sauce
2 tablespoons peanut oil
2 shallots, chopped finely
2 cloves garlic, minced
1 stalk lemongrass (white portion), chopped finely
3 tablespoons carrot, peeled and chopped
3 tablespoons frozen sweet peas, thawed
3 tablespoons frozen corn, thawed
½ cup barbecued pork, chopped
1 (6-inch) lap cheong (dried Chinese sausage)
3 cups cooked rice, cooled
½ tablespoon fresh lime juice

Directions
1. In a small bowl, beat the eggs with ⅛ teaspoon of fish sauce. Set aside.
2. In a skillet, heat 1 tablespoon of oil over medium-high heat and cook the egg mixture for 2–3 minutes, stirring continuously.
3. Transfer the scrambled eggs onto a plate and set aside.
4. In the same skillet, heat the remaining oil over medium heat and sauté the shallots, garlic and lemongrass for 2–3 minutes.
5. Add the carrot, peas and corn and stir fry for about 1 minute.
6. Add the pork and sausage and stir fry for about 1 minute.
7. Add the rice and remaining fish sauce and stir fry for 1–2 minutes.
8. Stir in the eggs and lime juice.
9. Serve hot.

Nutrition (per serving)
Calories 493, fat 18.3 g, carbs 55.2 g, sugar 4.7 g,
Protein 29 g, sodium 372 mg

Yangchow Fried Rice

A unique fried rice recipe for the whole family. Shrimp pairs nicely with rice, pork, peas and eggs.

Serves 6 | Prep. time 15 minutes | Cooking time 13 minutes

Ingredients
4 ounces frozen medium shrimp, thawed, peeled and deveined
½ teaspoon cornstarch
Salt and pepper as required
5 tablespoons canola oil
6 ounces roast pork, chopped
1 medium yellow onion, chopped
½ cup frozen peas, thawed
4 cups cooked rice, cooled
3 large eggs, beaten lightly

Directions
1. In a bowl, toss the shrimp in the cornstarch, salt and pepper to coat well.
2. In a skillet, heat 1 tablespoon of oil over medium heat and stir fry the shrimp for about 2 minutes.

3. Push the shrimp to the side of the skillet and stir fry the pork for 1–2 minutes.
4. Transfer the shrimp and pork to a plate.
5. In the same skillet, heat 2 tablespoons of oil over medium heat and sauté the onion for 3–4 minutes.
6. Add the peas and stir fry for about 2 minutes.
7. Transfer the onion and peas onto a plate.
8. In the same skillet, heat the remaining oil over medium heat and stir fry the rice for 1–2 minutes.
9. Add the beaten egg and cook for about 2 minutes, stirring continuously.
10. Add the shrimp, pork, onion, peas, salt and pepper and cook for about 1 minute.
11. Serve hot.

Nutrition (per serving)
Calories 414, fat 20.6 g, carbs 32.6 g, sugar 1.7 g,
Protein 22.4 g, sodium 666 mg

Spicy Malaysian Green Beans Fried Rice

A delicious and flavorful fried rice recipe with a Malaysian touch, this dish is prepared with dried shrimp, carrots, green beans, eggs, and fried chili paste.

Serves 3 | Prep. time 15 minutes | Cooking time 15 minutes

Ingredients
⅓ cup dried shrimp, rinsed
3 tablespoons vegetable oil
2 cloves garlic, minced
1 tablespoon fried chili paste
4 ounces green beans, cut into 1-inch pieces
1 small carrot, peeled and chopped finely
4 cups cooked rice, cooled
2 tablespoons soy sauce
2 large eggs

Directions
1. Soak the dried shrimp in warm water for about 10 minutes.
2. Drain the shrimp and chop them roughly.

3. In a large skillet, heat the oil over medium heat and stir fry the shrimp for 2–3 minutes.
4. With a slotted spoon, transfer the shrimp onto a plate.
5. In the same skillet, sauté the garlic for about 30 seconds.
6. Stir in the fried chili paste.
7. Add the green beans and carrots and cook for 2–3 minutes, stirring frequently.
8. Stir in the cooked rice and soy sauce.
9. With the spatula, create a well in the center of the rice mixture.
10. Crack the eggs into the well and then stir them into the rice mixture.
11. Cook for 4–5 minutes, stirring frequently.
12. Stir in the shrimp.
13. Serve hot.

Nutrition (per serving)
Calories 522, fat 19.3 g, carbs 61.5 g, sugar 3.3 g,
Protein 24.1 g, sodium 800 mg

Malaysian Fried Rice

A recipe for traditional Malaysian fried rice flavored with soy sauce, lime juice and veggies.

Serves 4 | Prep. time 15 minutes | Cooking time 27 minutes

Ingredients
1⅓ cups water
1 cup long-grain rice
1 large onion, chopped finely
3 red chilies, seeded
1 (1-inch) piece fresh ginger, peeled
2 cloves garlic, peeled
4 tablespoons fresh coconut, grated (divided)
2 tablespoons sesame oil
3 tablespoons fresh green peas
3 tablespoons carrot, peeled and chopped
3 tablespoons fresh corn kernels
1½ tablespoons light soy sauce
1 teaspoon sugar
Salt as required
2 teaspoons fresh lemon juice
Pepper as required

Directions
1. In a saucepan, bring the water and rice to a boil over medium-high heat.
2. Reduce heat to low and simmer, covered, for 9–10 minutes or until all the water is absorbed.
3. Remove from heat and leave the saucepan covered for 10–15 minutes.
4. Grind the onion, red chilies, ginger, garlic and 2 tablespoons of coconut until smooth. Set aside.
5. In a heavy-bottomed pan, heat the oil over medium heat and stir fry the peas and carrot for 2–3 minutes.
6. Add the corn and stir fry for about 1 minute.
7. Stir in the onion mixture and cook for about 5 minutes, stirring frequently.
8. Stir in the cooked rice, remaining coconut, soy sauce, sugar, salt and pepper and cook for 2–3 minutes.
9. Serve hot.

Nutrition (per serving)
Calories 379, fat 10.3 g, carbs 66.8 g, sugar 7.7 g,
Protein 8.6 g, sodium 252mg

Shrimp Fried Rice

A restaurant-quality fried rice recipe prepared with seasoned shrimp, eggs and vegetables.

Serves 4 | Prep. time 15 minutes | Cooking time 13 minutes

Ingredients
Sauce
2 tablespoons fish sauce
2 tablespoons soy sauce
2 teaspoons chili sauce
½ teaspoon shrimp paste
1 teaspoon sugar
Pinch of pepper

Fried Rice
2½ tablespoons peanut oil (divided)
¼ cup onion, minced
3–4 cloves garlic, minced
3–4 tablespoons white cooking wine
8–12 medium shrimp, peeled and deveined
2 large eggs
4 cups cooked rice, cooled

½–¾ cup frozen mixed vegetables (peas and carrots)

Directions
1. To make the sauce, in a bowl, mix together all of the sauce ingredients. Set aside.
2. To make the rice, in a skillet, heat 2 tablespoons of the peanut oil over medium-high heat and sauté the onion and garlic for about 1 minute.
3. Add the cooking wine and stir fry for about 2 minutes.
4. Add the shrimp and stir fry for 2–3 minutes.
5. Push the shrimp to the side of skillet.
6. Add the remaining peanut oil and increase heat to high.
7. Crack the eggs into the oil and cook for about 1 minute, stirring continuously.
8. Stir in the rice and frozen vegetables.
9. Drizzle the sauce over the rice mixture and cook for 4–6 minutes, tossing frequently.
10. Serve hot.

Nutrition (per serving)
Calories 419, fat 12.5 g, carbs 49.2 g, sugar 2.8 g,
Protein 23.9 g, sodium 1614 mg

Shrimp Paste Fried Rice

A unique fried rice recipe for your luncheon table, this shrimp paste rice is topped with pork, eggs, green mango, lime and chilies.

Serves 3 | Prep. time 15 minutes | Cooking time 10 minutes

Ingredients
2 teaspoons cooking oil
1 egg, beaten
2 tablespoons dried shrimp
1 cup cooked pork, chopped
2 tablespoons palm sugar
1 tablespoon fish sauce
3 cups cooked rice, hot
½ tablespoon shrimp paste
½ cup green mango, peeled and shredded
2 chili peppers, chopped
¼ cup shallots, sliced thinly
1 lime, sliced

Directions
1. In a skillet, heat 1 teaspoon of oil over medium heat.
2. Pour in the beaten egg and cook for about 1 minute per side.
3. Transfer the egg to a plate and cut it into strips. Set aside.
4. In the same skillet, heat 1 teaspoon of oil over medium-low heat and stir fry the shrimp for about 2 minutes.
5. Add the pork, palm sugar and fish sauce and cook for 2–3 minutes.
6. Transfer the pork mixture to a plate.
7. Place the shrimp paste in a large microwave-safe bowl. Place the rice over the shrimp paste. Microwave for about 2 minutes, stirring occasionally.
8. Divide the rice onto serving plates and serve alongside the egg strips, pork, shrimp, mango, chili peppers, shallots and lime.

Nutrition (per serving)
Calories 410, fat 7.8 g, carbs 54.8 g, sugar 1-.4 g,
Protein 28.8 g, sodium 798 mg

Tom Yum Fried Rice

Tom yum fried rice is a popular menu item in Thai restaurants. A combo of galangal, lemongrass, and makrut lime leaves gives this recipe a fragrant and distinct aroma.

Serves 2 | Prep. time 15 minutes | Cooking time 8 minutes

Ingredients
2 tablespoons vegetable oil
3 makrut lime leaves
1 (3-inch) stalk lemongrass, sliced
1 (3-inch) piece galangal, sliced
10 medium shrimp, peeled and deveined
½ cup mushrooms, sliced
1¾ cups cooked rice
1 tomato, chopped
1–2 Thai chilies
2 tablespoons lime juice
1 tablespoon soy sauce
1 tablespoon fish sauce
1 teaspoon chili paste
1 teaspoon sugar

Directions
1. In a skillet, heat the oil over medium-high heat and stir fry the lime leaves, lemongrass and galangal for about 2 minutes.
2. Add the shrimp and mushrooms and stir fry for 2–3 minutes.
3. Add the rice and tomatoes and stir to combine.
4. Stir in the remaining ingredients and cook for 2–3 minutes, tossing frequently.
5. Serve hot.

Nutrition (per serving)
Calories 446, fat 16.4 g, carbs 42.4 g, sugar 4.6 g,
Protein 30.4 g, sodium 1400 mg

Kimchi Fried Rice

A wonderful recipe for Korean inspired fried rice. Cabbage kimchi is the key ingredient of this flavorful rice dish.

Serves 2 | Prep. time 15 minutes | Cooking time 7 minutes

Ingredients
2 tablespoons canola oil
2 green onions, trimmed and sliced
2 cloves garlic, minced
1 cup napa cabbage kimchi, drained and cut into bite-sized pieces
2 tablespoons kimchi juice
2 teaspoons gochujang (Korean chili paste)
½ tablespoon soy sauce
1¾ cups cooked rice, cooled
1 teaspoon toasted sesame oil
1 teaspoon white sesame seeds, toasted
Pepper as required
Dried seaweed strips for garnish

Directions
1. In a large skillet, heat the oil over medium-high heat and sauté the green onion along with the garlic for 1–2 minutes.

2. Add the kimchi and kimchi juice and cook for about 1 minute, stirring frequently.
3. Add the chili paste and soy sauce and cook for about 1 minute, stirring continuously.
4. Stir in the rice.
5. Reduce heat to low and cook for 1–2 minutes, tossing frequently.
6. Stir in the sesame oil, sesame seeds and pepper and toss to coat well.
7. Serve hot, garnished with seaweed strips if desired.

Nutrition (per serving)
Calories 365, fat 18.8 g, carbs 42.3 g, sugar 1.9 g,
Protein 6.6 g, sodium 1490 mg

Hibachi Fried Rice

Make this delicious restaurant-style hibachi fried rice for your family. This recipe features a mild taste of soy sauce and a prominent taste of butter.

Serves 4 | Prep. time 15 minutes | Cooking time 6 minutes

Ingredients
¼ cup butter
½ cup onion, cut into 1-inch cubes
2 teaspoons chopped garlic
¼ cup chopped carrots
¼ cup peas
2 eggs, beaten
4 cups cooked rice
1 tablespoon toasted sesame oil
1 tablespoon soy sauce
Salt as required
½ teaspoon ground white pepper

Directions
1. In a skillet, melt the butter over medium heat and stir fry the onion and garlic for about 1 minute.

2. Add the carrots and peas and stir fry for about 1 minute.
3. Push the vegetables to one side of the skillet.
4. Add the beaten eggs and cook for about 2 minutes, stirring continuously.
5. Mix the eggs with the vegetables.
6. Add the cooked rice, salt, white pepper, soy sauce and sesame oil and cook for 1–2 minutes, tossing frequently.
7. Serve hot.

Nutrition (per serving)
Calories 366, fat 17.6 g, carbs 43.8 g, sugar 1.8 g,
Protein 7.8 g, sodium 384 mg

SPICED RICE RECIPES

Malaysian Coconut Rice

A delicious Malaysian rice recipe, this coconut rice is served with anchovy chili sauce, fried anchovies, peanut, cucumber and hard-boiled egg.

Serves 8 | Prep. time 20 minutes | Cooking time 30 minutes

Ingredients
Rice
2 cups long-grain rice, rinsed and drained
2 cups coconut milk
2 cups water
1 (½-inch) piece fresh ginger, sliced thinly
1 whole bay leaf
¼ teaspoon ground ginger
Salt as required

Sauce
2 tablespoons vegetable oil
1 medium onion, sliced

3 shallots, sliced thinly
3 cloves garlic, sliced thinly
2 teaspoons chili paste
1 (4-ounce) package white anchovies, washed
¼ cup tamarind juice
3 tablespoons sugar
Salt as required

Serving
1 cup vegetable oil
1 cup raw peanuts
1 (4-ounce) package white anchovies, washed
4 boiled eggs, peeled and halved
1 cucumber, sliced

Directions
1. To make the rice, in a medium pan, stir together all of the rice ingredients over medium heat.
2. Cover and bring to a boil, then reduce heat to low and simmer for 20–30 minutes or until done.
3. Meanwhile, for the sauce, heat the oil in a skillet over medium heat and sauté the onion, shallots and garlic for 1–2 minutes.
4. Stir in the chili paste and cook for about 10 minutes, stirring occasionally.
5. Stir in the anchovies and cook for about 5 minutes, stirring occasionally.
6. Stir in the tamarind juice, sugar and salt and simmer for about 5 minutes, stirring occasionally.
7. To prepare for serving, heat the oil in another large skillet over medium-high heat and cook the peanuts for 1–2 minutes, stirring continuously.
8. With a slotted spoon, remove the peanuts to paper towels to drain.
9. In the same skillet, cook the anchovies for 1–2 minutes or until crisp, flipping frequently.
10. With a slotted spoon, remove the anchovies to paper towels to drain.
11. Divide the rice onto serving plates and serve alongside the peanuts, fried anchovies, eggs, cucumber, and sauce.

Nutrition (per serving)
Calories 714, fat 48.2 g, carbs 52.4 g, sugar 9.2 g,
Protein 20.2 g, sodium 1123 mg

Turmeric Rice

A popular rice dish from Southeast Asia regions, with a beautiful golden yellow color, this rice recipe is perfect for celebrating special occasions.

Serves 4 | Prep. time 10 minutes | Cooking time 25 minutes

Ingredients
2½ cups water
½ cup coconut milk
2 cups jasmine rice, rinsed and drained
3 fresh pandan leaves, tied together
1 stalk lemongrass, bruised
2 kaffir lime leaves
2 bay leaves
1 tablespoon ground turmeric
½ teaspoon salt

Directions
1. In a large pan, bring the water and coconut milk to a boil over medium-high heat.
2. Stir in the remaining ingredients. Reduce heat to low and simmer, covered, for about 20 minutes. Remove from heat and let stand, covered, for about 10 minutes.

3. Fluff the rice with a fork.
4. Serve warm.

Nutrition (per serving)
Calories 395, fat 7.3 g, carbs 74.8 g, sugar 1.1 g,
Protein 6.8 g, sodium 296 mg

Indonesian Spiced Rice

One of the easiest ways to prepare spicy rice, this rice dish is flavored with a combo of cinnamon, turmeric and broth.

Serves 8 | Prep. time 10 minutes | Cooking time 35 minutes

Ingredients
3 tablespoons vegetable oil
1 large onion, chopped
2 cloves garlic, crushed
2 jalapeño peppers, seeded and minced
2 cups long-grain white rice, rinsed and drained
1 teaspoon ground turmeric
½ teaspoon ground cinnamon
2 (14½-ounce) cans chicken broth
1 cup water
1 bay leaf

Directions
1. In a large, heavy-bottomed pan, heat the oil over medium heat and sauté the onion, garlic and jalapeños for about 8 minutes.
2. Stir in the rice, turmeric and cinnamon and cook for about 2 minutes, stirring continuously.
3. Stir in the broth, water and bay leaf and bring to a boil.
4. Reduce heat to low and simmer, covered, for about 20 minutes.
5. Remove from heat and let stand, covered, for about 5 minutes before serving.

Nutrition (per serving)
Calories 242, fat 6.1 g, carbs 38.6 g, sugar 1.3 g,
Protein 5.7 g, sodium 422 mg

GLUTINOUS RICE RECIPES

Sticky Rice

This steamed rice platter is one of the simplest ways to prepare sticky rice at home.

Serves 6 | Prep. time 10 minutes | Cooking time 30 minutes

Ingredients
2 cups glutinous rice, rinsed, soaked for 6 hours, and drained

Directions
1. Arrange a colander in a large pan of water.
2. Place the rice in the colander.
3. Bring the water to a boil over medium heat.
4. Cover and reduce heat to low.
5. Steam, covered, for about 10 minutes.

6. Flip the rice with a large spatula and steam, covered, for 10–20 minutes.
7. Serve warm.

Nutrition (per serving)
Calories 225, fat 0.4 g, carbs 49.3 g, sugar 0.1 g,
Protein 4.4 g, sodium 3 mg

Lotus Leaf Rice Wraps

A classic sticky rice recipe for special meals, these lotus leaf wraps are filled with sticky rice, chicken, Chinese sausages and vegetables.

Serves 8 | Prep. time 25 minutes | Cooking time 35 minutes

Ingredients
1 (6-ounce) boneless, skinless chicken breast, cut into small cubes
2 tablespoons Chinese rice wine (divided)
2½ teaspoons cornstarch (divided)
¼ teaspoon salt
1¼ cups glutinous rice, soaked for 1 hour and drained
4 dried black mushrooms, soaked in hot water for 20–30 minutes and drained
1 tablespoon water
1 tablespoon light soy sauce
1 teaspoon dark soy sauce
2 tablespoons vegetable oil
1 clove garlic, chopped
2 Chinese sausages, sliced finely
Pepper as required
¼ teaspoon sesame oil
4 lotus leaves, cut in half, soaked in hot water for 1 hour, drained and dried

Directions

1. In a bowl, toss the chicken cubes with 1 tablespoon of wine, 1 teaspoon of cornstarch and salt to coat well.
2. Refrigerate to marinate for 20–25 minutes.
3. Line a bamboo steamer with parchment paper. Add the rice.
4. Half-fill a large skillet with water.
5. Arrange the steamer over the water, not touching it.
6. Bring the water to a boil over medium heat.
7. Cover and steam the rice for about 20 minutes.
8. Remove the rice from the steamer and set aside, covered, to keep warm.
9. Meanwhile, drain the mushrooms and then squeeze out any excess water. Remove the stems of the mushrooms and then chop them finely. Set aside.
10. In a small bowl, dissolve the remaining cornstarch in the water.
11. In another small bowl, add the remaining wine and both soy sauces.
12. Add the cornstarch mixture and beat until well combined. Set aside.
13. Filling: In a skillet, heat the vegetable oil over medium heat and sauté the garlic for about 30 seconds.
14. Add the chicken cubes and stir fry for 3–4 minutes.
15. Add the sausages and mushrooms and stir fry for about 1 minute.
16. Stir in the sauce mixture.
17. Stir in the pepper and cook for 1–2 minutes, stirring continuously.
18. Remove from heat and stir in the sesame oil. Set aside to cool.
19. Wraps: Divide the rice and filling into 8 portions.
20. Arrange the lotus leaves on a smooth surface.
21. Place 1 portion of rice in the center of each lotus leaf. Top with the filling mixture.
22. With your hands, shape the rice to forms a ring around the filling.
23. Form a square parcel with the lotus leaf and then tie it with twine.
24. Arrange the lotus parcels on a heatproof plate.
25. Again, half-fill the large skillet with water.
26. Arrange the steamer over the water, not touching it.
27. Place the plate of wraps in the steamer.
28. Bring the water to a boil over medium heat.
29. Cover and steam for about 15 minutes.
30. Serve warm.

Nutrition (per serving)
Calories 238, fat 10 g, carbs 26 g, sugar 1 g,
Protein 11 g, sodium 299 mg

Crispy Rice

A Thai crispy rice recipe for a deliciously addictive snacking treat that's easy to prepare.

Serves 2 | Prep. time 10 minutes | Cooking time 8 minutes

Ingredients
2 cups cooked jasmine rice, chilled in the refrigerator for 1 day
2 tablespoons canola oil
1½ tablespoons Thai chili paste
2 teaspoons soy sauce
2 teaspoons lime juice

Directions
1. In a large bowl, mix together the cooked rice and oil.
2. Heat a skillet over medium heat.
3. Add the rice and spread in a single, even layer.
4. Cook without stirring for 4–5 minutes or until the bottom is a light golden brown.
5. Stir in the chili paste and soy sauce, breaking the rice up into bite-sized bits.
6. Stir in the lime juice and remove from heat.

Nutrition (per serving)
Calories 374, fat 15.9 g, carbs 49.9 g, sugar 3.1 g,
Protein 5.1 g, sodium 343 mg

Rice Balls

Pearl balls are a fun finger food made with sticky rice and ground pork.

Serves 15 | Prep. time 20 minutes | Cooking time 35 minutes

Ingredients
¾ cup glutinous rice, soaked overnight and drained
1 pound ground pork
2 water chestnuts, minced
1 large green onion, minced
1 large egg white
1 tablespoon light soy sauce
1 tablespoon dry sherry
1 teaspoon salt
Pepper as required

Directions
1. Spread the drained rice onto a baking sheet and set aside.
2. In a large bowl, mix together the remaining ingredients.
3. Make small balls with 1 tablespoon of pork mixture each.
4. Roll the meatballs in the glutinous rice to coat completely.

5. Arrange the balls on a heatproof plate.
6. Bring a large pan of water to a boil over medium heat.
7. Arrange the steamer over the water without touching it.
8. Place the plate of balls in the steamer.
9. Cover and steam for 25–35 minutes or until completely done.
10. Serve warm.

Nutrition (per serving)
Calories 86, fat 1.1 g, carbs 8.9 g, sugar 0.1 g,
Protein 9 g, sodium 90 mg

Japanese Fried Rice Cakes

A recipe for rice cakes that are great as snacks or appetizers. These Japanese rice cakes are a true example of deliciousness.

Serves 2 | Prep. time 15 minutes | Cooking time 9 minutes

Ingredients
2 cups cooked Japanese rice
2 tablespoons all-purpose flour
1 tablespoon dry seaweed flakes
2-3 tablespoons vegetable oil

Directions
1. In a bowl, mix the the cooked rice, seaweed flakes, and flour until well combined.
2. Make small, round, flat cakes from the rice mixture.
3. In a skillet, heat the oil over low heat and fry the rice cakes for 2–3 minutes.
4. Carefully flip the rice cakes and fry for about 2 minutes more.
5. Flip the rice cakes again and increase heat to medium.
6. Fry for 1–2 minutes per side or until crispy and golden.
7. Serve warm.

Nutrition (per serving)
Calories 258, fat 7.2g, carbs 42.7 g, sugar 0 g, Protein 4.3 g, sodium 0 mg

Mango Sticky Rice

A delicious dessert treat from classical Thai cuisine, this sticky rice is steamed, mixed with thick coconut cream and sugar, and then paired with sweet mango.

Serves 6 | Prep. time 15 minutes | Cooking time 41 minutes

Ingredients
1½ cups glutinous rice, rinsed
1⅓ cups unsweetened coconut milk, stirred well (divided)
⅓ cup + 3 tablespoons sugar (divided)
¼ teaspoon salt
1 tablespoon lightly toasted sesame seeds
1 large mango, peeled, pitted and sliced

Directions
1. Soak the rice in a bowl of water overnight.
2. Arrange the rice in a steamer over a large, deep saucepan of simmering water.
3. Cover with a kitchen towel and then tightly with a lid.
4. Steam the rice for 30–40 minutes or until tender, adding more water if necessary.

5. Meanwhile, in a small saucepan, bring 1 cup of coconut milk, ⅓ cup of sugar and the salt to a boil, stirring continuously.
6. Remove from heat and set aside, covered, to keep warm.
7. Remove the rice from heat and transfer into a large bowl.
8. Add the coconut milk mixture and stir to combine.
9. Cover and set aside for about 30 minutes or until the coconut milk mixture is absorbed.
10. To make the sauce, in a small pan, cook the remaining coconut milk and sugar for about 1 minute, stirring occasionally.
11. Transfer the sauce to a bowl and refrigerate to chill.
12. Divide the rice onto serving plates and drizzle with the sauce.
13. Garnish with sesame seeds and serve with mango slices.

Nutrition (per serving)
Calories 401, fat 14 g, carbs 66.7 g, sugar 27.5 g,
Protein 5.3 g, sodium 108 mg

Black Sticky Rice Pudding

Black rice pudding is a healthy recipe that's perfect for dessert! This black rice is flavored with coconut milk, brown sugar and whipped cream.

Serves 6 | Prep. time 10 minutes | Cooking time 1 hour 20 minutes

Ingredients
20¼ ounces coconut milk (divided)
1½ cups water
1 cup black glutinous rice, soaked overnight and drained
¼ cup brown sugar
¼ teaspoon salt
3 large eggs
2 tablespoons whipped cream

Directions
1. In a pan, bring 14 ounces of coconut milk to a boil with the water, rice, brown sugar and salt.
2. Cook, partially covered, for 45–50 minutes or until all the liquid is absorbed.
3. Remove from heat and set aside to cool.
4. Preheat oven to 350°F (177°C).

5. In the pan of rice, mix in the remaining coconut milk and eggs.
6. Spread the rice mixture evenly into a baking dish.
7. Cover and bake for about 30 minutes.
8. Remove from the oven and set aside, uncovered, to cool slightly.
9. Serve warm topped with whipped cream.

Nutrition (per serving)
Calories 406, fat 27.1 g, carbs 36.2 g, sugar 9.3 g,
Protein 7.7 g, sodium 151 mg

SUSHI RECIPES

Sushi is a delicious way to eat a meal based on rice and different ingredients. The best things is that it's easy to make at home with a little practice. Below find the basic steps of making sushi rolls.
In Japan, sushi refers to vinegar rice with raw fish or other basic ingredients wrapped in nori or seaweed "paper." Another version, *nigiri*, is a hand-shaped bite-sized portion of rice with a dash of wasabi and a thin slice of raw fish on top. The origin of sushi is traced back to Southeast Asia, where fish was stored in rice as a mean of preservation. Through China, sushi was eventually introduced in Japan, during the 8th century. It was a street food that could be eaten quickly with the hands, an ancient kind of fast food. Here are basic instruction to make sushi at home.

Basic Steps in Making Sushi

Here are some basics equipment and ingredients you will use for making sushi.

Basic Equipment
- sushi rolling mat
- sharp, non-serrated knife
- rice cooker
- plastic wrap
- cutting board

Basic Ingredients
- nori (edible sheets of dried seaweed)
- sushi rice
- raw fish and other seafood (should always be sashimi-grade), meat, vegetables, fruit
- sushi condiments (there is a wide variety including soy sauce, wasabi, pickled ginger, mayonnaise, Sriracha, and many more)

Here are the steps for making sushi:

1. Prepare the nori sheet

Line the rolling mat with a sheet of plastic wrap (this will help in shaping and storing the roll). Place one full sheet of sushi nori on the lined sushi rolling mat, shiny side down.

2. Spread with sushi rice

Cover the nori sheet with prepared sushi rice, leaving the last inch and a half (away from you) bare. Use plastic gloves or moisten your hands with a solution of water and a little vinegar called tezu to prevent the rice from sticking (recipe below).

NOTE: **To make an inside-out roll,** *cover the rice layer with a sheet of plastic wrap. Lifting with the bottom plastic wrap, turn over the nori onto the bamboo rolling mat. Remove top plastic wrap.*

3. Place the filling

Place ingredients for the filling crosswise over the rice-covered nori.

4. Roll

Fold the mat over, to roll the sushi. Apply firm pressure while rolling to make a tight roll.

5. Tighten the roll

Moisten the flap of uncovered nori and roll over it to seal. Repeat rolling to tighten the roll, if necessary. Be careful not to roll the plastic wrap into the sushi.

6. Slice the roll

Use a sharp, non-serrated knife and run cold water over the blade to keep the nori and rice from sticking. Do not use a sawing motion as this would tear the nori. To get even slices, begin slicing at the center of the roll then proceed to cut each piece at the center as well. Cut into 8 small pieces or 6 larger pieces.

Thick Sushi Roll (Futomaki)

*Serves 4 | Prep. time 30 minutes plus 30 minutes cooling time
Cooking time 15 minutes (for sushi rice)*

Ingredients
3 sheets nori
15-20 large shrimp, cooked
3 pieces imitation crab sticks, halved lengthwise
⅓ cup carrot, finely grated
1 small Japanese cucumber, cut into strips
1 avocado, pitted, peeled, cut into strips
2 leaves romaine lettuce, shredded
4 cups cooked rice, seasoned with sushi vinegar
¼ cup rice vinegar
Wasabi, soy sauce, and sushi ginger (*gari*), as condiments

Sushi rice
3 cups sushi rice (shari)
4 ¼ cups sushi vinegar (recipe below)

Sushi vinegar
3 ½ cups water
½ cup of rice vinegar (do not use any other vinegar)
2 tablespoons white sugar

2 teaspoons refined salt

Vinegar water for dipping hands (Tezu)
¼ cup water
2 teaspoon rice vinegar

Directions
For sushi vinegar
1. Combine all the sushi vinegar ingredients in a saucepan and warm it on the stovetop over medium heat. Stir until the well dissolved. (You may also heat the vinegar solution in the microwave.)
2. Put the rice in a fine-mesh strainer and wash under cold running water until the rinsing water runs clear. Drain well.

Sushi Rice - on the stovetop
3. Place the rice in a heavy-bottomed pot and add the water. Make sure the rice surface is level. Bring it to a boil, reduce the heat to low, and cover the pot. f the boiling liquid overflows, remove the lid for it to go down and replace the lid immediately. Allow the rice to absorb all the water. Watch out for scorching. If you smell the rice burning, immediately remove it from the heat and allow it to cook in residual heat. The rice is done when all water has been absorbed.

Sushi rice - using a rice cooker
4. Place the washed rice grains in the rice cooker pot and add the 3 ½ cups of water. Cook according to the rice cooker's instructions (usually you just press the "cook" button).
5. Transfer the cooked rice to a hangiri, or a large mixing bowl, and place it in the refrigerator to cool. At this stage, fillers can be prepared while waiting for the rice to cool down.
6. Make sure the rice is completely cool, as the center may still be hot.
7. Pour the vinegar mixture over the rice and mix it into the rice with your hands.

To make the roll
1. As you will make 3 rolls, divide all the ingredients into 3.
2. Follow the steps for making sushi described before. When placing the filling: a) arrange 5-6 shrimp in a row about 2" from the close edge. b) add a row of sea sticks, then a row of shredded lettuce. c) on top of the shrimp, place slices of avocado and shredded, stacked like logs of wood. d) roll
3. Cut each roll into 8 slices. Serve with soy sauce, wasabi, and pickled ginger.

Nutrition (per serving)
Calories 322, fat 1 g, carbs 70 g, sugar 25 g,
Protein 5 g, sodium 1519 mg

Dragon Roll

Serves 4 | Prep. time 1 hour

Ingredients
For filling
2 avocados, halved, pitted, peeled, sliced thinly crosswise
½ lemon (optional), to squeeze on the avocados to prevent browning
2 nori sheets, cut in half crosswise
2 cups prepared sushi rice
1 Japanese cucumber, pitted, cut lengthwise into 8 pieces
8 pre-cooked shrimp tempura
⅛ cup fish roe or *tobiko,* plus more for garnish
Grilled eel *or unagi* (optional)

For toppings
Spicy mayo (Japanese mayo mixed with Sriracha or hot sauce to taste)
Unagi Sauce (store-bought)
Green onion, sliced for garnish

Directions
1. Gently press the avocado slices with your fingers and then with the side of a knife to make them malleable. Sprinkle with lemon, if using.
2. Follow the steps for making sushi. You'll be rolling it inside out.
3. After turning the roll inside out, put the cucumber strips, shrimp tempura, *tobiko,* and *unagi* (optional) at the bottom end of the nori sheet.
4. Roll it up. After you are done rolling, BEFORE CUTTING, place the avocado slices on top to look like a dragon's "scales."
5. Cover with plastic wrap and place the mat over the roll. Squeeze gently to make the avocado wrap over the top of the roll.
6. Cut the roll into 8 slices.
7. Top each slice with a bit of roe. Drizzle with spicy mayo and sprinkle sliced green onions
8. Serve with *unagi* sauce.

Nutrition (per serving)
Calories 520, fat 13 g, carbs 78 g, sugar 30 g,
Protein 19 g, sodium 868 mg

Nigiri Sushi

Serves 6 | Prep. time 30 minutes | Freezing time 1 hour

Ingredients
4-6 ounce piece sushi-grade tuna or salmon
About 3 cups prepared sushi rice
Wasabi
Tezu solution, for washing hands

Directions
1. If using salmon, cover the fish with salt and leave it for 1 hour.
2. Rinse off the salt and put the salmon into the freezer until it is completely frozen.
3. Defrost until it is easy to slice.
4. Slice the fish very thinly, about ¼ inch thick and the size of a domino.
5. Dip hands into the tezu.
6. Take a scoop of sushi rice to fit your fist. Pack the rice in your fist to make a small rectangle of sushi rice.
7. Dab one side of the fish slices with wasabi and place it, wasabi side down, on the sushi rectangle.
8. Serve with more wasabi, soy sauce, and sushi ginger.

Nutrition (per serving)
Calories 56, fat 1 g, carbs 8 g, sugar 0 g,
Protein 3 g, sodium 193 mg

Vegetarian Nigiri

Serves 6 | Prep. time 30 minutes

Ingredients
Sushi rice
1 small zucchini, sliced very thinly (paper-thin)
1 slice small green *shiso* or *perilla*, cut lengthwise and in small diagonal strips
¼ *nori* seaweed, cut into about ¼-inch wide strips
Wasabi
Salt
Sushi vinegar
Hot sauce

Directions
1. Sprinkle the zucchini slices generously with salt. Rub it in, and leave it to sit until the turnip has wilted. Rinse and drain, and squeeze out the water.
2. In a wok, warm the oil and quickly stir-fry the zucchini. Remove from wok and place on paper towels to absorb excess fat.
3. Take a scoop of sushi rice to fit your fist. Pack the rice in your fist to make a small rectangle.
4. Smear on a dab of wasabi paste, and place piece of *shiso* leaf on top.

5. Dip 2-3 slice of zucchini in sushi vinegar, lay it on the rice, and adjust the shape.
6. Wrap a strip of nori like a belt around its width, tucking the ends underneath.
7. If desired, place a dab of hot sauce on top and serve.

Spicy Tuna Maki

Serves 4-6 | Prep. time 15 minutes

Ingredients
4 sheets nori, cut in half crosswise
2 cups sushi rice
Sushi ginger
Wasabi
Soy sauce

For filling
5 ounces ahi tuna (yellowfin or bigeye), *Sashimi*-grade, finely chopped
2 tablespoons green onions, minced
2 tablespoons mayonnaise
1 tablespoon hot sauce

Directions
1. Combine the ingredients for the filling in a bowl and mix well.
2. Follow the steps for making sushi up to step 3.
3. For the filling, spoon a thin line of the tuna mixture down the center of the rice.
4. Proceed up to step 5 (do not cut yet).

5. Before cutting, remove the plastic wrap and set the roll aside, covering with a damp cloth while you work to finish the remaining rolls.
6. Cut the roll in half, then into thirds so each roll results in 6 pieces.
7. Serve with sushi ginger, wasabi, and soy sauce.

California Maki

Serves 8-10 | Prep. time 30 minutes

Ingredients
5 sheets nori
1 large cucumber, peeled, seeded, cut lengthwise into long strips
2-3 avocados, halved, pitted and cut into thin strips
Freshly squeezed lemon juice
Imitation crab sticks, cut lengthwise
Wasabi
Sesame seeds, if desired

Directions
1. Sprinkle the avocado with lemon juice to prevent browning.
2. Follow the steps for making sushi for an inside-out roll, up to step 3.
3. For the filling, arrange the strips of avocado and cucumber along the center of the rice, and top with crab meat.
4. Proceed with succeeding steps up to step 5 (do not cut yet)
5. Wrap the plastic wrap around the roll and set aside until ready to cut. Refrigerate for longer storage. Repeat with remaining nori sheets to make additional rolls.
6. Roll in sesame seeds if desired. Cut into 6-8 rolls as desired.
7. Serve with wasabi, soy sauce, and sushi ginger.

Vegetable Maki

Serves 6-8 | Prep. time 30 minutes

Ingredients
1 package nori roasted seaweed sheets
2 carrots, peeled and sliced lengthwise into narrow strips
1 cucumber, pitted and sliced lengthwise into narrow strips
1 avocado, halved, pitted and cut into narrow strips
Cream cheese (block form), cut into narrow strips
Soy sauce
Wasabi for serving
Sesame seeds

Directions
1. Follow the steps to making sushi up to step 3.
2. For the filling, place a carrot strip, cucumber strip, cream cheese, and avocado across the rice bed.
3. Proceed with the rest of the steps in making sushi.
4. Garnish each piece with sesame seeds.
5. Serve with soy sauce for dipping and wasabi.

RECIPE INDEX

HOMEMADE NOODLES RECIPES — **11**
   Hand-Pulled Noodles — 11
   Rice Noodles — 13
   Egg Noodles — 15
   Ramen Noodles — 17
   Udon Noodles — 19

NOODLE RECIPES — **21**
   Chicken Lo Mein — 21
   Chicken Chow Mein — 23
   Shrimp Lo Mein — 25
   Shrimp Chow Mein — 27
   Stir-Fried Chicken Noodles — 29
   Fried Noodles — 31
   Singaporean Noodles — 33
   Lan Zhou Beef Noodles — 35
   Dan Dan Noodles — 37
   Vegetable Chow Mein — 39
   Calamari with Noodles — 41
   Korean Japchae Noodles — 43
   Stir-Fry Udon Noodles with Shrimp — 45
   Chinese Sesame Noodles — 47
   Chinese Zha Jiang Mian Noodles — 49
   Filipino Pancit Canton — 51
   Chicken Pad Thai — 53
   Beef Pad See Ew — 55
   Mongolian Chicken Noodles — 57
   Malaysian Kl-Hokkien Mee Noodles — 59
   Taiwanese Beef Noodles Soup — 61
   Chinese Beef Noodles Soup — 63
   Thai Drunken Noodles — 65
   Beef Pho — 67
   Chinese Hot Sauce Noodles — 69

CONGEE RECIPES — **73**
   Simple Congee — 73
   Chicken Congee — 75
   Pork Meatballs Congee — 77
   Fish Congee — 79

FRIED RICE RECIPES — 81
- Fried Rice — 81
- Chicken Fried Rice — 83
- Vietnamese Fried Rice — 85
- Yangchow Fried Rice — 87
- Spicy Malaysian Green Beans Fried Rice — 89
- Malaysian Fried Rice — 91
- Shrimp Fried Rice — 93
- Shrimp Paste Fried Rice — 95
- Tom Yum Fried Rice — 97
- Kimchi Fried Rice — 99
- Hibachi Fried Rice — 101

SPICED RICE RECIPES — 103
- Malaysian Coconut Rice — 103
- Turmeric Rice — 105
- Indonesian Spiced Rice — 107

GLUTINOUS RICE RECIPES — 109
- Sticky Rice — 109
- Lotus Leaf Rice Wraps — 111
- Crispy Rice — 113
- Rice Balls — 115
- Japanese Fried Rice Cakes — 117
- Mango Sticky Rice — 119
- Black Sticky Rice Pudding — 121

SUSHI RECIPES — 123
- Basic Steps in Making Sushi — 123
- Thick Sushi Roll (Futomaki) — 128
- Dragon Roll — 131
- Nigiri Sushi — 133
- Vegetarian Nigiri — 135
- Spicy Tuna Maki — 137
- California Maki — 139
- Vegetable Maki — 140

APPENDIX

Cooking Conversion Charts

1. Measuring Equivalent Chart

Type	Imperial	Imperial	Metric
Weight	1 dry ounce		28 g
	1 pound	16 dry ounces	0.45 kg
Volume	1 teaspoon		5 ml
	1 dessert spoon	2 teaspoons	10 ml
	1 tablespoon	3 teaspoons	15 ml
	1 Australian tablespoon	4 teaspoons	20 ml
	1 fluid ounce	2 tablespoons	30 ml
	1 cup	16 tablespoons	240 ml
	1 cup	8 fluid ounces	240 ml
	1 pint	2 cups	470 ml
	1 quart	2 pints	0.95 l
	1 gallon	4 quarts	3.8 l
Length	1 inch		2.54 cm

* Numbers are rounded to the closest equivalent

2. Oven Temperature Equivalent Chart

Fahrenheit (°F)	Celsius (°C)	Gas Mark
220	100	
225	110	1/4
250	120	1/2
275	140	1
300	150	2
325	160	3
350	180	4
375	190	5
400	200	6
425	220	7
450	230	8
475	250	9
500	260	

* Celsius (°C) = T (°F)-32] * 5/9
** Fahrenheit (°F) = T (°C) * 9/5 + 32
*** Numbers are rounded to the closest equivalent

Printed in Great Britain
by Amazon